Future-Focused Learning

10 Essential Shifts *of Everyday Practice*

Lee Watanabe-Crockett

Solution Tree | Press
a division of
Solution Tree

555 North Morton Street
Bloomington, IN 47404
800.733.6786 (toll free) / 812.336.7700
FAX: 812.336.7790

email: info@SolutionTree.com
SolutionTree.com

Visit **go.SolutionTree.com/instruction** to download the free reproducibles in this book.

Printed in the United States of America

Library of Congress Cataloging-in-Publication Data

Names: Crockett, Lee, author.
Title: Future-focused learning : ten essential shifts of everyday practice /
   Lee Watanabe Crockett.
Description: Bloomington, IN : Solution Tree Press, [2018] | Includes
   bibliographical references and index.
Identifiers: LCCN 2018001296 | ISBN 9781945349584 (perfect bound)
Subjects: LCSH: Holistic education. | Problem-based learning. | Problem
   solving--Study and teaching. | Interdisciplinary approach in education.
Classification: LCC LC990 .C76 2018 | DDC 370.11/2--dc23 LC record available at https://lccn.loc.
gov/2018001296

Solution Tree
Jeffrey C. Jones, CEO
Edmund M. Ackerman, President

Solution Tree Press
President and Publisher: Douglas M. Rife
Editorial Director: Sarah Payne-Mills
Art Director: Rian Anderson
Managing Production Editor: Kendra Slayton
Senior Production Editor: Todd Brakke
Senior Editor: Amy Rubenstein
Copy Editor: Miranda Addonizio
Proofreader: Jessi Finn
Text and Cover Designer: Abigail Bowen
Editorial Assistant: Sarah Ludwig

Acknowledgments

With gratitude to Simon, Jackie, Kathleen, and Andrew for continuing to challenge my thinking and challenge me to do more and Todd for his insightful capacity to translate the intentions behind my writing. Mostly thank you to Mia for her immeasurable contributions to my work and life.

Solution Tree Press would like to thank the following reviewers:

Melanie Gates
Director of Secondary Education
    for STEM
Middleborough Public Schools
Middleborough, Massachusetts

Joshua Giebel
Mathematics Facilitator
Columbus Signature Academy
New Tech High School
Columbus, Indiana

Beth Johnson
K–12 Technology Instructional Specialist
Broken Arrow Public Schools
Broken Arrow, Oklahoma

Brandon Johnson
Principal
STEAM Middle School
Burleson, Texas

Colleen McKay
Assistant Superintendent for Curriculum
    and Instruction
Cook County School District 130
Blue Island, Illinois

Laura Sexton
Spanish Teacher
Gaston Early College High School
Dallas, North Carolina

Renée Williams
Assistant Superintendent for Instruction
Honeoye Falls-Lima Central
    School District
Honeoye Falls, New York

Table of Contents

Reproducible pages are in italics.

Chapter 7

Chapter 8

Chapter 9

Chapter 10

Appendix

Visit **go.SolutionTree.com/instruction** to
download the free reproducibles in this book.

About the Author

Lee Watanabe-Crockett is an optimist. He believes in a bright future and our ability to build it together through connection and compassion. He works with governments, education systems, international agencies, and corporations to help people and organizations connect to their highest purpose and realize their wishes for the future.

Lee believes in creating balance in the reality of a digital present and future. As such, living in Japan, he studies Aikido, Buddhism, and the Shakuhachi, a traditional Japanese bamboo flute. Joyful curiosity is the foundation of his approach to creating vital learning environments for groups around the world.

His several best-selling books, including *Literacy Is NOT Enough*, *Growing Global Digital Citizens*, and *Mindful Assessment*, have garnered many awards and are used in schools and universities around the world.

To learn more about Lee's work, visit https://globaldigitalcitizen.org or www.leewatanabecrockett.com, or follow @leecrockett on Twitter.

To book Lee Watanabe-Crockett for professional development, contact pd@SolutionTree.com.

Introduction

Many of education's most popular authors and keynote speakers seem to speak of little else than what is wrong with education. The constant dialogue on *why* with so little discussion of *how* fatigues me, and I also believe most educators are weary of hearing what they are doing wrong. In 2011, I decided to no longer discuss the problem without presenting a solution. In the void, I put forward the essential fluencies as a solution, and I have been amazed how quickly they have spread through systems around the world. These fluencies, which represent essential future-focused (21st century) skills, include solution fluency, information fluency, creativity fluency, media fluency, collaboration fluency, and global digital citizenship, and I first published about them with Ian Jukes and Andrew Churches in *Literacy Is NOT Enough* (Crockett, Jukes, & Churches, 2011). The truth is, we developed these fluencies as a response to a much broader consideration, a question that we have posed to thousands of educators all over the world; that question is, "What are the most crucial skills our students need to live and succeed in the transforming world of both the present and the future?"

I believe if we are to achieve positive transformation, we need to focus on a bright future and work together to create it. I assume that you are reading this book because you want to know precisely what that change looks like and how to get there. As such, I will not take time to discuss the *why* in this book, but only the *how*. I do this by pinpointing ten core shifts of practice—practices rooted in future-focused learning and the essential fluencies—that you can implement with your learners regardless of your established teaching pedagogy. I support these shifts with many details and examples.

It is the hard work of teachers working to shift their practice with the essential fluencies that keeps me committed to support them with my work. I hope this book contributes to the positive work you are doing and your relentless desire to improve. So, before we begin, it is important to understand how the shifts of practice I present in this book fit into many popular teaching pedagogies, how these ideas connect to future-focused learning, and how I've organized this book so you can make the best use of it.

The Missing Piece in Popular Pedagogical Approaches

For some years, many schools have used the idea of problem- and project-based learning by bringing into classes and subjects real-world, contextual, and relevant projects. For the most part, these are single-subject approaches. For example, the International Baccalaureate Group 4 subjects have students in various disciplines within the sciences work collaboratively to investigate a problem ("IB Group 4 Subjects," n.d.). These approaches are beneficial since they bring in a series of processes that enable students to address problems and develop projects. Other examples include Apple's ongoing support for challenge-based learning (Digital Promise, n.d.), the Buck Institute's support for project-based learning (Buck Institute for Education, n.d.), and so on.

Similarly, the science, technology, engineering, and mathematics (STEM) initiative is a cross-curricular approach to integrating some of the sciences, namely the traditional sciences, mathematics, technology and applied technology, and science in the form of engineering. STEM originated in the United States as a solution for dwindling numbers of graduates in these disciplines (U.S. Department of Education, n.d.).

An evolution of STEM is the science, technology, engineering, arts and design, and mathematics initiative (STEAM), which adds aesthetic and design considerations in the form of art to bring together function and form. STEAM represents the next evolutionary step of STEM (STEM to STEAM, n.d.).

Although all of these pedagogical approaches are laudable and beneficial, none actually address the bigger focus. The real world, except for academia, does not divide itself up into neat compartments or disciplines. A technology company does not employ only technologists. It brings together a raft of different skill sets that span all the disciplines we have at school and more. For example, to develop a new product you absolutely need the engineers, technologists, and mathematicians but you also need the following.

- The artists and designers who make the product both functional and aesthetically suitable

- The economists who examine the financial viability of the solution

- The historians who understand the framework that the problem is set in and who consider the prior developments and frameworks that may or will impact the solution

- The wordsmiths and linguists who develop and present the proposals, arguments, manuals, media releases, and press kits and packaging that accompany any product

- The media experts who fashion the messages into social media, traditional media, and so on
- The legal experts who investigate and protect the concepts, intellectual property, and copyright
- The environmental scientists who consider the impact and significance of the development on our environment
- The social scientists who develop understanding of the society the company is producing the solution for and consider the psychological aspects of the design that make it more appealing and functional (This includes considering the cultural impacts, significance, and importance of not only the problem but the solution.)

The list is obviously extensive, but it clearly involves more than just a single-subject discipline. It encompasses and embraces all aspects of a holistic education, and it highlights why our end goal should not be project-based learning, STEM, or STEAM, but rather the holistic integration of all aspects of learning—both formal (the disciplines we teach) and informal (the portable and applicable skill sets)—into the following aptitudes.

- Finding, identifying, and defining real-world, relevant problems
- Understanding the origins, significance, impact, and worthiness of those problems
- Developing creative and ethical solutions that embrace the skills, passions, and abilities of a broad group of learners (both students and staff), experts, and the wider community
- Engendering the synergy among the different learning areas to develop products and solutions greater than the combined input of the disciplines

To achieve these aims requires us to undertake a number of different actions by developing schoolwide approaches to problem solving, research, collaboration, and ethics. This is why Andrew Churches and I developed the essential fluencies. These essential fluencies codify the kind of work Andrew and I do in hundreds of schools in a dozen countries to help learners strive together to solve real-world problems that matter and create a bright future for all.

I cannot stress enough that pedagogies like project-based learning, STEM, design thinking, and many others all have their value. Some of them have an almost cult-like following, largely because as teachers shift to these pedagogies, their classrooms transform, learning comes alive, and outcomes improve. I call this *professional transformation*: the moment at which a teacher realizes the benefits from a shift in practice and will never go back.

This doesn't mean these pedagogies don't represent commodities; and like any commodity, each seems to have its own packaging, marketing, and following. To support them, various stakeholders hold conferences and workshops, provide supplies, establish resources, and even design furniture labeled for them. This is not a criticism of these fine approaches. If you successfully implement one or more of them in your school and learners benefit, then I applaud you for your commitment and encourage you to continue the great work you are doing. I offer the ideas in this book for you to consider as ways to take that great work and make it exceptional by engaging in future-focused learning.

Shifts to Future-Focused Learning

Future-focused learning is a holistic (school- or systemwide) approach in which learners strive together to find and solve real-world problems that matter; they focus beyond the curriculum with the goal of gaining an interlinked real-world education and cultivating capabilities essential to ensure their success beyond school.

A common issue I encounter when consulting with schools is change fatigue. Teachers often challenge a new initiative in its early stages if it is another *direction du jour* or if it requires an actual commitment. This occurs because schools bring to their educators so many ideas they tout as *the answer* only to cast them aside in favor of a newer initiative or just let them dissolve over time. On more than one occasion, a teacher has expressed concern to me that every time the principal goes to a conference, it means a new idea will return with a huge but short-lived push that soon becomes a memory. This is a valid concern and significantly impacts teacher buy-in to any process. I've managed to overcome this with many schools by focusing on the ten shifts of practice I present in this book. You can implement these future-focused practices in your classroom regardless of core pedagogy; they don't reset your practice, but rather support it.

One of the key reasons these shifts work is that the sheer scale of a new teaching initiative can be massive, and the effort required to launch it exhausting. A teacher who has been comfortable and reasonably successful with delivering content in a teacher-centered environment might be able to see the validity of a new pedagogy in learner outcomes but find it too big a change to consider.

In fact, it was in working with a teacher who was quite overwhelmed with high anxiety and fear of change that I first began to think about these shifts. He told me that using solution fluency was just too much for him to consider and he would leave teaching if he had to make this kind of change. Unfortunately, many teachers are in the same position of fatigue and fear. I wished that there were a few simple things—simple *microshifts*—that I could use to slowly help teachers to transform.

I asked him if, at the beginning of each lesson, he would be willing to engage in one small change (a microshift) by clearly presenting and discussing his learning intentions (learning goals) with his learners along with providing them with clear success criteria. Very quickly, his learners started to excel and asked what tomorrow's learning intentions were, then what they were for the entire week. Soon learners were arriving in his class having already met the success criteria. Eventually, he no longer needed his carefully planned lessons because students had already moved beyond them. Upon seeing this success, he asked me what to do next; we started working with essential questions, which became his next shift of practice.

After this experience, I started using these shifts of practice with all my clients and going deeply into solution fluency with the ones who were keen and felt ready to take on this challenge as they had been incrementally successful with other shifts. By offering a range of shifts for everyone to work on, I was in fact personalizing the learning for the teachers. Which is, of course, one of the shifts I present in this book!

Structure and Use of This Book

This book presents ten core shifts of practice you can use with your students immediately, regardless of your core curriculum or instructional pedagogy. Each chapter presents a future-focused shift, explains what it is, and shows how it benefits learning. These ten shifts are as follows.

1. **Essential and herding questions:** Providing learning without an essential question is like offering food to people who are full—they won't accept it if they aren't hungry. Essential questions stimulate students' appetite for learning. For this shift of practice, challenge yourself to incorporate essential questions in every learning activity.

2. **Connection through context and relevance:** Ask yourself where your students may come across a certain kind of information or a specific skill in their lives outside of school. If it's something they'll come across in their own world, then instantly there is a connection that brings relevance and context to the learner.

3. **Personalized learning:** Learning is personal, and it becomes more personal when students have a personal connection to the task. By engaging in future-focused learning, endless possibilities appear for personalization. It could be the task, the learning process, the research, the assessment, the evidence of learning created, or the role in collaboration.

4. **Challenge of higher-order-thinking skills:** Take it up a notch or two using Bloom's revised taxonomy by shifting your learning tasks to higher-order-thinking tasks (Anderson & Krathwohl, 2001). Challenge your

learners to evaluate and create instead of demonstrating remembering and understanding.

5. **Information fluency for research skills:** We are bombarded with information every second of our lives. We assess the information and, in a split second, determine how it will affect us and our decisions. Information-fluency skills slow down this process so we can dissect every aspect of assessing information and learn how to do it better. It is a fluency built for maximizing the usefulness and credibility of all forms of research.

6. **Process-oriented learning:** Use other essential fluencies as the learning process to challenge learners to solve real-world problems that matter, dive deep into inquiry, or create something amazing. The microshifts in this chapter feature uses for solution fluency, media fluency, and collaboration fluency.

7. **Learning intentions and success criteria:** Whether working in one subject or across multiple key learning areas, the impact of being transparent with curricula is amazing. No matter if it's curriculum lists, learning intentions, standards, or objectives, putting them out front for the benefit of your learners is an essential shift in future-focused learning.

8. **Learner-created knowledge:** *Learner creation* means learners are creating new knowledge as part of a learning task, a new product, or a new solution. It's also about developing the evidence of learning as well as the criteria.

9. **Mindful assessment:** Mindful assessment is *fair, clear, transparent, deliberate*, and *purposeful*. It enhances learning by focusing on formative assessment as well as reflecting on the learning process. We must rethink the bond between teaching and learning by assessing the crucial skills our learners need to thrive in life beyond school, as embodied by the essential fluencies. We do this through the practice of mindfulness with both assessment and feedback for improvement.

10. **Self- and peer assessment:** Reflection on learning is a skill we can internalize and grow with by practicing it during our school years. That's why encouraging learner reflection through self- and peer assessment adds such a powerful dimension to learning. Self- and peer assessment stress and reinforce the importance of collaboration, reduce workload, and increase engagement and understanding. In addition, learners' insights and observations become highly valued since they help them reflect on and understand the processes of their own learning.

Within each chapter, you will find three specific microshifts that detail specific activities you can engage your students in along with reflective questions for you to consider after trying them. I call them microshifts because each is a single activity that can help nudge your practice toward a permanent transformation in relation to the broader shift of practice. Each chapter concludes with a series of guiding questions for further reflection or for a book study with your colleagues or learning community.

Finally, the book's appendix also presents additional microshift ideas for you to consider, seven small shifts of practice you can implement to further each core shift in this book. All in all, this book contains one hundred microshifts that you can immediately use in your classroom.

As you work through this book, or after you complete it, I recommend starting with the low-hanging fruit by considering only one of these shifts. Reflect on the microshifts and additional microshift ideas and either choose one or develop your own microshift to trial. You might choose whichever shift is easiest to implement or the one you are most excited about. When you do this, consider what you hope to see happen beforehand and afterward, and reflect on whether this occurred or if a different outcome occurred, be it favorable or unfavorable. You may then choose to adjust your approach and attempt it again. Eventually, through a process of application, debriefing, and adjustments, you will find that the shift becomes more entrenched in your practice and improves learning outcomes. When this happens, move to whichever shift you want to explore next.

Although I do focus this text on communicating to you as an individual, it's important to understand that I developed these shifts of practice as a way to assist entire faculties to transform their learning. As such, these shifts are particularly well suited to teams. As a group, you can identify a shift, collectively implement it using multiple microshifts, and reflect on its outcome by working together to quickly identify what elements and processes lead to success with your unique learners and learning environments. When using these shifts as a group, note that because they overlap and interrelate heavily, not everyone has to work on the same shift. Having each member work on a different shift of practice as an alternative to everyone working on the same shift also leads to rich professional conversations.

For example, with my clients, I work the shifts through a continual action-research cycle. We assign a *learning conversation facilitator* to a group of teachers. These facilitators may be administrators, heads of faculties, learning coaches, or any other authority figure who makes sense in your organization. What is most important is a structured process with accountability.

The facilitator meets with each teacher to identify the following: Which shift will you undertake? How will you trial it with your learners? What key indicators of success are you looking for? By when will you accomplish these indicators? The final step before adjourning is to set the follow-up meeting based on the timeline the teachers have set for themselves.

Each teacher then works to implement the shift and collect evidence of success. At the follow-up meeting, teachers reflect on the evidence they collect based on the key indicators for success they identified in the initial meeting. After discussion, the facilitator works with the teacher group to determine the next steps, and the cycle repeats until both the teachers and the learning conversation facilitator agree to move to a different shift.

To help facilitate this kind of work, my organization developed a new application platform (Wabisabi, https://wabisabizen.com). If you opt to try it out, I recommend that you access the Professional Growth section, which documents this process. The valuable content in this section is a direct result of the effort and outcomes of transforming teaching practices using these shifts.

It doesn't matter which shift you implement first, only that eventually you work through them all. By focusing on these shifts, you will transform education from explicit teaching to future-focused learning for your learners, one microshift at a time.

chapter 1

Essential and Herding Questions

The first shift I present in this book involves deeply engaging students with their learning. You can do this by forming an *essential question* that tasks them with examining a learning topic beyond the surface level. You can then use their initial, free-form responses to that question to form a series of *herding questions*—questions that help drive them toward the specific learning goal you have in mind. Let's explore what makes a question essential by looking at the concept from a different angle and then how you can follow that with herding questions.

When presenting new learning, consider this: If this learning is the answer, what was the question? Often, educators present learning as the next thing students need to know or be able to do. As educators, we may understand the scope and sequence that makes the learning essential, but students may have no idea. I believe the presence of an essential question might actually be *essential* to learning.

I have found that deep questioning leads to exceptional thinking when answers prompt more questions and more in-depth inquiry. Key learning areas arise when students face a flurry of essential questions that drive them to investigate; the fruits of that investigation result in knowledge, understanding, and insight. Would biology exist had someone not asked, "What are the fundamental elements of living systems? What structures exist within, and what purpose do these structures serve?"

I find that learning usually springs from a need or from curiosity about a personal connection. Learning has a reason; it is an answer. Without a question, learning lacks both purpose and meaning and is lost. All learning should start with an essential question, and the relatively brief time it takes to discuss an essential question benefits learners in terms of engagement, context, and relevance. Getting students' initial answers to an essential question also provides you with insight into what they think and already know. Furthermore, the essential question and the conversation around it reveal personal connections, which provides the opportunity to personalize learning, something we discuss in chapter 3 (page 35).

For example, perhaps the curriculum you want to address involves medicine and diseases. An essential question you might ask students is, "How best can we ensure everyone's health?" In reply, students may talk about obesity, nutrition, or healthy eating. They may discuss exercise, safe streets, or bicycle helmets. It doesn't matter which direction the conversation takes, as long as they all engage in dialogue and debate. Even though they are a long way from where you intended (medicine and diseases), you can use their ideas and the engagement you established to ask a series of herding questions such as, "If all that works, and you're living a healthy lifestyle and wearing a bike helmet, what happens if you suddenly become ill? What happens if you get a disease? Do you know anyone who has ever had a terminal illness?"

This creates an entirely new line of conversation, and eventually, you can arrive at medicine and the eradication of diseases. In the process, however, you have identified several opportunities for planning your next unit and glimpsed ways to personalize learning by allowing students to approach the content through what was relevant to them. For example, learners may know the pain and trauma of having someone close to them with a terminal illness, and questions that are relevant to them based on this experience stimulate a drive in them to find answers.

Put simply, the essential question is what starts the debate; the herding questions are what you (the facilitator) use to fuel the debate and drive it faster and more furiously toward a particular line of questioning. You are like the sheepdog steering the sheep through a narrow gate. The first nip from the sheepdog is the essential question to get the sheep moving. The herding questions manage their direction. In this chapter, I establish what attributes make a question essential and then explore some microshifts of practice you can use to stir students' engagement.

Characteristics of an Essential Question

A good essential question calls for higher-order thinking, such as analysis, inference, evaluation, and prediction. Recall alone cannot answer it, and it points toward important, transferable ideas within (and sometimes across) disciplines (Wiggins & McTighe, 2005). I define an essential question as having the following characteristics.

- It has no obvious answer and is not answerable with a simple search.

- It goes beyond topic or skills (skills relevant to life beyond school and to students' interests).

- It creates the opportunity to use herding questions through the *hydra effect* (cut off one head [question], and two more appear).

- It's timeless and naturally recurs throughout the ages (it is as relevant in Plato's time as it is today).

- It requires critical and continual rethinking (the deeper into the inquiry, the less certain the answer).

- It inspires meaningful discussion, debate, and knowledge development.

- It engages learners through a personal connection.

An essential question leads learners to explore the background of an issue and choose from various plans, strategies, or possible courses of action to generate a complex, applicable solution. A truly essential question inspires a quest for knowledge and discovery, encourages and develops critical-thinking processes, and is all about possibilities rather than the definitive. From here, I will help guide your understanding of what makes a question essential and how you can evolve and develop a good essential question to use with your learners.

From Nonessential to Essential

Consider this question: Do rainstorms create moisture? Then, ask yourself the following questions: "Does this question inspire contemplation or any serious inquiry? Does it generate other questions and ideas or meaningful discussions? Does it motivate the learner to think about creating something to solve a problem or meet a challenge?"

Not really. It's a relatively empty question. It is nonessential.

In class, educators often ask students questions like, "How do rainstorms create rain?" This question is a bit better. It calls for some investigation and a search for knowledge. The problem is that students can answer it very quickly with some light research and a one-paragraph answer or a diagram. They did learn something, but they didn't have to actually discover or create anything.

A further evolution might be to ask, "How does the rain from rainstorms benefit ecosystems?" In students, this question gives rise to deeper thinking, broader questions, and more in-depth research. Through this process, learners discover how storms affect different systems, and this will lead them to other considerations. It's a fine question, but does it inspire, engage, and push them to visualize? Is it as good as it could be? How can we take this even deeper into authentic inquiry and creativity and make it into a quest for engineering a solution to an intriguing problem?

What about asking, "How best could we thrive without the rain from rainstorms?" Now we've got something *really* essential that will inspire students to fully engage with their learning. It also leads naturally to forming herding questions to help drive student explorations where they need to go, such as, If rainfall suddenly stopped for all time, what would it mean to life on Earth, human and otherwise? Who and what would an absence of rain specifically affect? Think about ecosystems, agriculture and food production, business, and the beauty of nature itself; how would all these things change?

Imagine the ingenious and creative solutions to this problem your students might come up with!

Development of an Essential Question

Although the previous example can help you better understand what an essential question is and looks like, and how to refine an existing question to be one, it doesn't demonstrate how you might create one in the first place. Over the years of developing essential questions with teachers, I have facilitated conversations about essential questions on a whiteboard, crossing out parts of the sentence and rewriting them underneath. The usual frustrated response I hear from teachers is that it looks so obvious when I do it. This led me to consider what the simplest method is to consistently develop a quality essential question and herding questions. While I was poring over photos of various whiteboards from different facilitation sessions, I realized I have a very particular and unconscious two-step approach in which I consider the questions, (1) How do I move the question as high up Bloom's revised taxonomy (Anderson & Krathwohl, 2001) as possible? and (2) How do I remove specificity? It's simplest to illustrate with an example, so consider the following question.

Who was Tony Abbott?

This is not a great question for all the reasons we established in the previous section. So, let's simply get on with the first step of moving it up Bloom's taxonomy as high as possible. Let's revise.

Was Tony Abbott or Gough Whitlam the better prime minister?

This question now requires evaluation in the form of comparing and contrasting, which puts it near the top of Bloom's taxonomy (Anderson & Krathwohl, 2001). It would, however, be simple to create a response and most likely would not engage learners nor inspire earnest debate. Next, let's begin by removing the specificity of the two prime ministers.

What makes a great prime minister?

At this point, the evaluation is much deeper, causing the learner to develop a set of criteria based on personal judgments. We can, however, continue to remove specificity.

What makes a great leader?

This question still requires students to intensely evaluate and develop criteria, but it inspires much more inquiry as many more herding questions arise from it. What makes a great leader at school, or in a family, or on a sports team, or in an army, or in a spiritual sense? Are these characteristics the same, and what factors influence their importance? Although this question is excellent, we can even go one step further.

What is greatness?

This is a truly essential question. Notice that each previous question is a subset of this question; in other words, each question becomes less and less specific as it develops. In speaking of greatness in general, we could be considering great leaders, great humans, or great devotion to sacrifice or humility. Learners can run wild with this kind of question, allowing you to achieve engagement and then add specificity back in to herd them where you want to go. If you are teaching students about historical leaders, a subset of herding questions might be to ask about heads of state, of which a further subset might be prime ministers, and ultimately a particular individual. As herding questions become more specific, they drive the conversation closer to the original and often curriculum-related question. In other words, they work backward from the essential question of "What is greatness?"

I find that educators are often concerned with asking such a huge, open question because they can't see how it relates back to the content they are teaching. By starting with a specific question, moving it up Bloom's taxonomy (Anderson & Krathwohl, 2001), and then removing specificity, it creates opportunities for you to ask a series of herding questions that act like breadcrumbs leading back to the beginning. If learning is an answer, then it is the essential question that begins the process.

Before I address some microshifts of practice, a final point I'd like to add is a simple tip that helps in the construction of essential questions. Consider the question words *who*, *what*, *where*, *when*, *why*, and *how*. Which of these might best assist in the formation of an essential question? If you reflect on the levels of Bloom's revised taxonomy (Anderson & Krathwohl, 2001), *who*, *what*, *where*, and *when* are knowledge-based questions, typically found at the bottom levels of the taxonomy. (They are the lower-order-thinking skills.) *How* correlates with analysis, and *why* with evaluation, which are at the top. (They are higher-order-thinking skills.) In general, *who*, *what*, *where*, and *when* support the *why* and the *how*. The reason my example of "What is greatness?" works is because the consideration of greatness itself requires extensive evaluation and justification, whereas a question such as "What is the square root of four?" does not.

Microshifts of Practice: Essential and Herding Questions Create Engagement

There are a variety of approaches you can take in developing and using essential and herding questions to engage students in your classroom. In this section, I describe three methods: (1) explore the essential, (2) go beyond the curriculum, and (3) use Socratic seminars. Each section includes a specific activity you can use with students and reflective questions you can ask yourself about how your students responded.

Explore the Essential

The first step in being able to create essential questions is understanding what they are, and part of this comes from being able to recognize one when you see it. Often a question may seem essential, but on closer inspection, you will come to realize that it can be even broader and help students incorporate even more critical thinking and knowledge creation into their answers. By recalling the characteristics of essential questions I present in this chapter, along with the examples I provide, you can create an exercise whereby you and your learners both learn to spot essential questions on the fly and understand what makes them so.

Activity

Begin by discussing what essential questions are with your learners and challenge them to analyze and understand their structure and significance to meaningful learning—that is, independent thinking and learning skills that will stick with them and remain useful throughout their lives. Depending on your students' grade level, you can ask your learners questions such as the following.

- "What do you believe makes a question essential?"
- "What makes them different from simple or closed questions?"
- "Where do we see such questions asked in the world outside school?"
- "When are essential questions important to ask?"
- "How would you go about building an essential question right now?"
- "What are some examples of essential questions that are famous and well known?"
- "Why are essential questions vital to success in so many areas of life?"
- "How does asking essential questions shape and affect our views, opinions, and ideas about things?"

One simple exercise you can use is to collect examples of both essential and nonessential questions and place them where the whole class can see them. Next, have learners indicate on a worksheet or by using voting cards which questions they believe are essential and which ones are not, and have them discuss their perceptions in groups.

You can take this activity even further by discussing with your students how they could transform nonessential questions into essential questions. Ask them what it takes to turn a simple question with an elementary answer into one that fosters meaningful discussion, exploration, and reflection. Ask them how they would transform the question in both word and intent.

Reflection

After you complete this activity with your students, take some time to reflect on and answer the following questions.

- What knowledge were your learners able to demonstrate about essential questions?

- How much better do they now understand an essential question's structure and importance?

- In what ways and in what other kinds of activities could your students apply this new knowledge?

Go Beyond the Curriculum

In *Understanding by Design*, Grant Wiggins and Jay McTighe (2005) remind us that essential questions are "important questions that recur throughout all our lives" and that they are "broad in scope and timeless by nature" (p. 108). Such questions lead us to explore the deeper issues of life and what it means to have uniquely human experiences and interactions with the world around us and those we share it with. These issues may not necessarily align with your core curriculum, but there is value in having your students receive practice with how to explore them. This is the time for you to step outside the curriculum and encourage them to let their imaginations soar without fear of judgment. Ask your learners what's on their minds, what their primary concerns are, and what they truly wonder about.

Activity

Have your learners think about, write, and revise a list of questions that concern the kinds of timeless topics that interest them and make them want to investigate. This is a way for you to connect them to their interests, their deepest musings about everything under the sun, and perhaps even to things beyond the sun. They need not restrict the questions they write to curriculum, although the next step would be finding ways to use herding questions to connect them with it in ways that are creative, challenging, and relevant.

The essential questions you ask students for this activity can be from a variety of different viewpoints. They can be personal.

- "How do you discover your true calling?"

- "What can you do to improve your relationship with your family?"

- "Which country have you always wanted to visit and why?"

They can be philosophical.

- "What does it mean to truly be alive?"
- "Why do we dream and what do our dreams tell us?"
- "What should be our greatest goal as a society and why?"

They can be ethical.

- "Is condemning a murderer to death justifiable?"
- "Is it acceptable to risk harm to others to benefit someone who is clearly in need?"
- "Should people be allowed to clone themselves?"

They can be scientific.

- "What type of diet allows for optimum athletic performance?"
- "When and how do scientific theories change?"
- "How can we be sure that the universe beyond our world is truly infinite?"

They can be global.

- "How could we ensure and sustain enough food, water, and clothing for every living person on Earth?"
- "How has technology transformed how we see ourselves and others? Is this good or bad?"
- "How can small actions eventually change the world?"

For a deeper challenge, break students into groups and have them take turns posing their essential questions to the group for discussion. Pay careful attention to the questions they are sharing, and if possible, encourage them to find ways to link them to lessons in the curriculum. From there, choose the best questions as the focus for upcoming classroom units of study.

Reflection

After you complete this activity with your students, take some time to reflect on and answer the following questions.

- What are the types of issues that students revealed they are most interested in exploring?
- Why are these matters important to them?
- How did student groups discuss and answer the questions?
- Is there anything students are still wondering about?
- What do they know about exploring important issues in this manner that they didn't know before?

Use Socratic Seminars

The Greek philosopher Socrates was renowned for his belief in the power of asking good questions. The aptly named Socratic seminar seeks to provide a powerful platform for students to both ask and answer open-ended questions about a wide range of topics and content in a way that is highly collaborative and social ("Socratic Seminar," n.d.). Socratic seminars call for students to apply critical and independent thinking by way of forming both essential and herding questions about the discussion topic and responding to the questions of others. Socratic seminars also teach learners how to respond to questions with thoughtfulness and civility.

Activity

Hold your own classwide Socratic seminar on a topic or material you choose. Begin by exploring the structure of the Socratic seminar with your learners. Students can prepare well beforehand by reading the appropriate text and formulating questions as though they were entering a formal debate. Work with students to also come up with a clear list of guidelines and expectations for the seminar.

On the day the seminar begins, you are the one best prepared to lead the discussion so that students can get their feet wet with the whole process. However, you ultimately want them to take over the proceedings and lead the discussions themselves, almost as if you weren't even in the room. Since your learners' thought processes and inquiries are the focal point of the Socratic seminar, it makes sense to involve students in these structural decisions.

The guidelines you'll agree to follow are important, such as when to turn discussion— a sharing of ideas—into debate. In this context, that debate should consist of peers attempting to persuade each other and challenge each other's opinions. Throughout the process, your role will be one of mediator and guide for the discussion, steering it back to the right trajectory if it should happen to go off the rails.

As you should always do when engaging students in a format of this nature, debrief afterward. You and your students work together to assess the effectiveness of the seminar on the day's or the week's learning goals. As part of this debrief, ask students to set goals for future seminars and discuss topics of interest that will provide fodder for lively discussions and the development of more essential questions.

Reflection

After you complete this activity with your students, take some time to reflect on and answer the following questions.

- What did the Socratic seminar teach learners about developing thinking and questioning skills?

- What were some of the most powerful moments for you and your students in this activity?

- What could the students have done differently to make the seminar more effective?

- How could you use this activity for assessment purposes?

Summary

Questions matter; they are, in fact, essential. Where there are no questions, there is no interest and no curiosity. Without interest, there is no learning. I believe that the art of teaching has less to do with knowing and more to do with questioning. Essential and herding questions lie at the root of powerful learning; they take a student from zero interest in learning to finding real answers and cultivating a desire to create meaningful solutions. Asking questions instead of simply providing answers moves the responsibility for the learning where it should be—to the student. Now that you know more about how to bring essential questions into your lessons every day, use your new knowledge to answer students' questions with more questions and let them reap the benefits. Asking questions that drive curiosity and interest is a tactic that you'll find incredibly useful when diving into our next shift of practice, which is all about connecting students to learning using context and relevance.

Guiding Questions

As you reflect on this chapter, consider the following five guiding questions.

1. Why do we ask questions?

2. What are essential and herding questions, and why are they important for learning?

3. What is the difference between a nonessential question and an essential one? In what ways can you use both to create a successful learning environment?

4. Why is it helpful to explore essential questions that lie outside your core curriculum?

5. How can you use Socratic seminars in your classroom to help students use essential and herding questions in ways that advance their learning?

chapter 2

Connection Through Context and Relevance

In this shift, I detail the importance of context and relevance to engaging students in their own learning. To give you a sense of why context and relevance are important to learning, I offer you an example from my own experience.

Living in Japan has been a tremendously rewarding and incredibly challenging experience for me. My language skills are fine for casual conversation, but I rely heavily on others for deeper conversations. To read and understand typical expressions and sentences in Japan, one must understand *hiragana*, *katakana*, and basic *kanji*.

The hiragana and katakana alphabets each contain 107 characters, which represent the sounds of Japanese and foreign words respectively. Beyond these, there are thousands of kanji, or Chinese characters. The set of kyōiku kanji, which students must learn by grade 6, alone contains 1,006 characters. Each of these can take twenty or more pen strokes to create, and learners must be able to write them with the correct stroke count, order, and direction as well as know their Japanese and Chinese readings. This is not a task most would want to undertake. It's probably also why none of my friends want to spend an evening with me. However, I am highly motivated and committed to this process, because I find the study fascinating and enlightening. Living in Japan, having non-English-speaking family and friends, and studying traditional arts, music, and Buddhism, all of which happen in Japanese, instill a high degree of relevance and motivate me to continue studying.

In order to learn something, it must stimulate your curiosity—in other words, interest comes before learning does. Connection and relevance occur when we stimulate an emotional response. Learners can be inspired, excited, curious, happy, or outraged as the result of a provocation, which, as the word means, provokes a response. Yes, even negative emotions can inspire decisive action in our learners. As educators, however, it is often our job to take a learner's negative energy and guide him or her toward turning it into something positive, specifically a positive action he or she can take toward solving a problem of consequence to the world.

In this chapter, I examine how emotion can create the necessary context and relevance in students, prompting engagement and interest in their own learning. I begin by thoroughly examining the scientific basis that connects emotion to learning engagement and then offer a series of microshifts of practice you can use in your classroom to connect students to their learning.

How Emotional Connections Establish Context and Relevance

Often, educators see relevance as something important for them to impart to learners. We may think limiting processed food and sugar is relevant to a teenager, but it is only our perception. If he or she does not perceive the relevance, then there is none. As educators, it is critical that we find a way to foster this connection. Students learn when they become emotionally engaged in conversations, ideas, and activities that have personal relevance to them (Immordino-Yang, 2015). The resulting emotional connection from personal relevance is what differentiates superficial, topical assimilation of material from a transformative education experience filled with mastery and deep learning, which is to say that students can apply their learning in different ways and under variable circumstances (Briggs, 2015).

Do not underestimate the connection emotion has to learning or interpret it as a trend, fad, or indulgence, which is a very human thing to do when confronted with a challenging concept or task. Creating this emotional connection might seem difficult, but research demonstrates that the investment in doing so is well worth it, resulting in significant increases in learning and academic performance (Lahey, 2014).

In "To Help Students Learn, Engage the Emotions" (Lahey, 2016), Mary Helen Immordino-Yang (2015) discusses her use of functional magnetic resonance imaging (fMRI), which reveals brain function in real time: "When students are emotionally engaged, we see activations all around the cortex, in regions involved in cognition, memory and meaning-making, and even all the way down into the brain stem."

Emotion is where learning begins or, as is often the case, where it ends. In *Emotions, Learning, and the Brain: Exploring the Educational Implications of Affective Neuroscience*, Immordino-Yang (2015) further states, "Even in academic subjects that are traditionally considered unemotional, such as physics, engineering or math, deep understanding depends on making emotional connections between concepts" (p. 18). Her most striking statement for me, though it seems like common sense, is something educators often overlook in their rush to deliver content: "It is literally neurobiologically impossible to think deeply about things that you don't care about" (Lahey, 2016).

Simply stated, if there is no emotional connection, learning doesn't happen. In my experience, compassion creates one of the strongest connections. When we see someone helpless, in distress from war or natural disaster, or in pain, our *ego* (our self) stills. In Japanese Buddhism, there is a word for this experience, *sesshin* (切心), which means to cut (切) the heart (心). Sesshin is the tingling sensation we feel at the tip of our heart when we become present to the suffering of another and feel his or her pain as our own pain, and it is a powerful gateway to relevance for learners. When we awaken to and selflessly respond to the needs of others, we realize our highest purpose. Service is the answer to the question, What room in my heart can I make for the suffering of others? While charity is often about collecting change, service is making change.

Finding this gateway with your students is actually pretty simple. For example, in October 2016 at Melrose High School in Canberra, my colleagues and I held the first-ever Solution Fluency Thinkfest. Five elementary schools sent grades 4 and 5 students to work with a high school student who acted as the facilitator. We tasked them with using solution fluency (Crockett & Churches, 2017) to research and develop a solution to the question, What is the most urgent problem in the world? (Note that I write much more about solution fluency in chapter 6 [page 77, Solution Fluency].)

Given the elementary students' young ages, I naively expected to hear concerns that they aren't allowed to play video games when they want or that they have too much homework. Figures 2.1 through 2.4 (pages 23–25) briefly list what is on the minds of these learners.

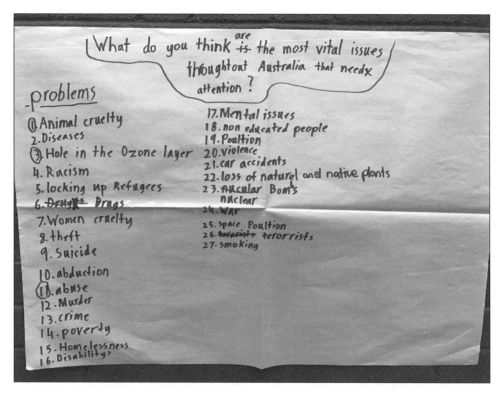

Figure 2.1: An elementary student lists vital issues facing Australia.

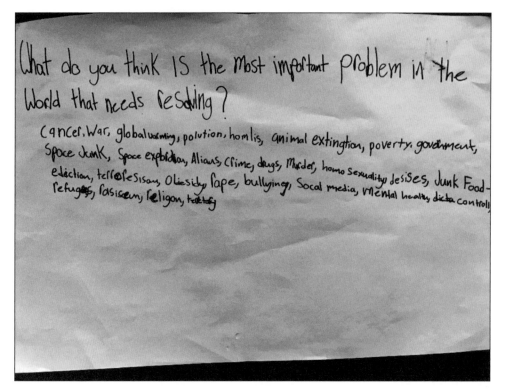

Figure 2.2: An elementary student lists vital issues facing the world.

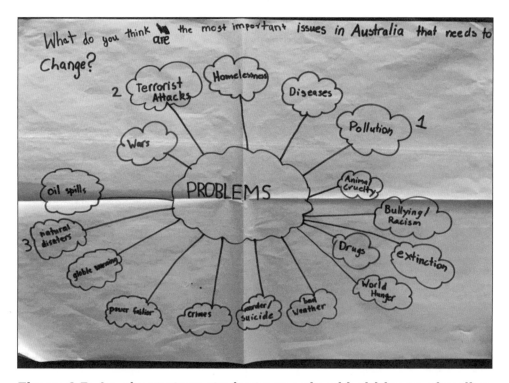

Figure 2.3: An elementary student uses cloud bubbles to visualize vital issues facing Australia.

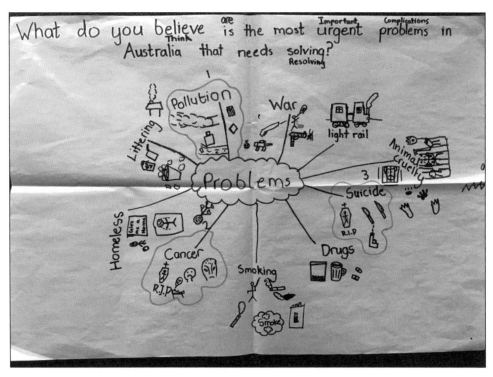

Figure 2.4: An elementary student illustrates problems Australia needs to resolve.

When we gave these students the freedom to express their true feelings, their responses shocked us all; and we are worried about literacy and numeracy and getting through the curriculum? Upon seeing the responses, we quickly met as a team and instead of panicking, which we were doing on the inside, calmly agreed that these were problems and that we shared their concerns. Note that our anxiety came not from what the learners were feeling, but strictly our own concern about how we were going to have this level of conversation with these learners and how we could realistically help them arrive at a solution to such concerns. It seemed impossible. But we reminded the team that solution fluency is what you do when you don't know what to do, and so to begin by defining the problem clearly.

The work the learners did that day inspired all of us. Once they were able to clearly state the problem, which is the *define* phase of solution fluency, they moved on to the second phase, *discover*. This phase is about researching, considering what one needs to know and to be able to do, and understanding what might have occurred in the past to cause this problem to exist. It also involves understanding what solutions, if applied in the past, might have prevented this from occurring and reflecting on whether those solutions are still applicable. The learners were so engaged in their conversation and research that we couldn't get them to stop for lunch. They presented potential solutions to many of these issues and demonstrated to me once again that we dramatically underestimate what our learners can do. For example, one group chose to develop a solution to war. Think about that for a moment. As adults, which of us would sit down in a group and actively try to understand the problem of war and develop a solution for it (in four hours, no less)? In the end, the group's solution was to develop and evenly distribute a single global currency so that there would be financial equality among all nations. They presented solid arguments as to how this would solve the problem. Whether their solution was viable or not is immaterial. What matters is that because they found the questions relevant and were able to contextualize them, they demonstrated a deep understanding of and insights into many real-world issues and channeled these into considerable critical, analytical, and creative thinking.

If we had the courage to do so, we could expand this one conversation into an entire year's worth of learning, and we could find many opportunities to apply the curriculum to the inquiry. Many of the schools I work with are doing just that, but it starts small, one lesson at a time, connecting the curriculum with relevance to the learner. Consider the problems the students listed in figures 2.1–2.4, and ask your students, as we did, what they feel are the most urgent problems in the world. Next, ask yourself how you can apply the answers you receive to your existing curriculum. The answers you develop could be your next unit of future-focused learning.

Microshifts of Practice: Context and Relevance Foster Connection

Using emotion to provide students with enhanced context and relevance for their learning is something you can easily do within the bounds of your existing curriculum. In this section, I describe three methods: (1) search the heart, (2) teach with technology, and (3) use student-designed assignments. Each section includes a specific activity you can use with students and reflective questions you can ask yourself about how your students responded.

Search the Heart

In this chapter, we discussed the elementary students who participated in an exercise at Melrose High School and the responses they had to what they felt were the most urgent problems in their country or the world that need immediate attention. This is proof positive that students care deeply about issues beyond what we may often assume to be their capabilities and concerns. What might your own learners be able to do?

For this microshift, you want to engage students in searching their hearts to increase their understanding of a problem and how to solve it. In so doing, your learners will establish the contextual understanding they need to make the content relevant to them.

Activity

Part of both understanding and solving a problem is having a deep awareness of why it is a problem in the first place. Pick a few topics concerning the world in general for the students to share in groups. Have them investigate the history of one or more global issues that humanity struggles with, and use the following questions to pinpoint why society has never been able to solve this problem. This entails students using both the *define* and *discover* stages of solution fluency, which you can read about in chapter 6 (page 75), as well as in *Mindful Assessment* (Crockett & Churches, 2017).

- Why do you feel we still suffer from these issues affecting our entire world stage?

- What actions have people and societies taken in the past, if any? Why have they not been successful?

- Who has responded primarily, and what have they been most vocal about?

- Who is in the strongest position to manage this issue most effectively and why?

- If left unchecked, what will this problem mean for us as individuals? For the community? For the world?

Next, have learners define one suggestion for a starting point to begin a change. They should be able to justify this choice either as a written response or orally to the whole class, whichever they think is best. Encourage them to explore what is possible as a best-case scenario by assuming that every resource they require to proceed is in place. This is a time for them to use the *dream* phase of solution fluency (Crockett & Churches, 2017) and imagine an outcome without restrictions or borders. The final stage is for students to work together to produce a theoretical timeline of events that begins at their starting point and continues to the fruition of their visualized outcome, highlighting all key points along the way.

Reflection

After you complete this activity with your students, take some time to reflect on and answer the following questions.

- What did students discover about these seemingly insurmountable issues in their research?

- How has the nature of these problems changed over time?

- How did they go about visualizing and designing their proposed outcomes?

- What did they learn about themselves and their ability to work together in this exercise?

Teach With Technology

Since the world has become interconnected through technology, and because technology is such a ubiquitous and highly integrated presence in our children's lives, it's increasingly necessary to involve technology in curricula by taking advantage of its abilities to foster collaboration, locate useful media and information, and develop creative solutions. We call technology we use in this way *edtech*, or educational technology ("Educational Technology," n.d.); the term encompasses both hardware (devices) and software (applications and other programs).

It's important to understand that integrating technology into your instruction doesn't mean that technology is going to supplant you. It is simply a means to enhance your practice. As a teacher, you are still a classroom's greatest resource, and having your students use digital devices in your classroom can provide you and your learners with an excellent teaching supplement that makes the learning more relevant for students while allowing you to spend more time on individual instruction.

To help you get started when considering ways to implement edtech in your school or classroom, consider the following three important strategies. Note that these strategies reflect both teacher and administrator concerns and represent only the beginning of the process when it comes to integrating technology with curricula.

1. **Scaffolding (incremental introduction of skills):** If you're interested in teaching with edtech, you've likely discovered a variety of tools that you want to share. But trying to do too much and introducing too many tools can stress you out, causing *analysis paralysis* and frightening off students and parents. To avoid this, begin by thoroughly researching and introducing one tool at a time. For example, administrators could have teachers become familiar with using Twitter (https://twitter.com) as a way to expand their personal learning networks. Teachers could have students use it as an avenue for quick quiz answers. (Similar to many social media and other digital platforms, Twitter requires all users to be at least age thirteen.)

   Before you begin, try establishing an online support team to keep you motivated and connected to learners and colleagues. Another great tool for making this happen comes from my own venture, Wabisabi (https://wabisabilearning.com), and my Solution Fluency Activity Planner (Global Digital Citizen Foundation, n.d.b). With the highly collaborative nature of this system, educators can find support from peers around the world who are doing great things. In addition, educators can use it to connect to other classes around the world so learners can learn from, with, and, more importantly, about each other.

2. **Clarity of purpose (how this applies to real-world practice):** For teachers, this means clarifying goals and being explicit in how you want to use the

tools for your own subjects. In other words, how is this tool relevant to you and what and how you are teaching with it? Take a look at the specific edtech tool, application, hardware, or online service you have your eye on and visualize how it can enhance your classroom and the learning that happens within it.

For administrators adopting schoolwide edtech or bring your own device (BYOD) initiatives, you must remember that teachers and students alike need support, especially when something is changing their routine. They must come away with a clear answer to the question, How does this new tool, application, hardware, or online service help me with learning or solve a problem within the class?

3. **Support (feedback and formative assessment):** Sometimes administrators work tirelessly raising funds to acquire the most expensive edtech tools and start the school year off using them regularly, only to let them gather dust for the rest of the year. Once you're in, you should be all in. Regular training sessions are a must. Beware the trap of offering only one professional development session at the beginning of the school year. Teachers will get *really* busy *really* quickly. If you can implement training so that it is unobtrusive, such as in the form of a formative assessment tool, all the better.

These three simple strategies mirror everything that educators and students need to successfully use edtech in the classroom. With them in place, you can begin to focus on specific technology-driven activities that help drive context and relevancy in students' learning.

Activity

Some specific activities for teaching with edtech can include using Twitter for quick quizzes and polls, using Facebook (https://facebook.com) for group-project management, and using LinkedIn (https://linkedin.com) to connect with industry professionals in the students' chosen field of interest. Decide which tools will enhance learning through direct experience for your learners. Here are six examples.

1. Digital portfolios (Evernote, https://evernote.com; Pinterest, https://pinterest.com; and Wabisabi, https://wabisabizen.com)

2. Assessment online (Socrative, https://socrative.com; Plickers, https://plickers.com; and Kahoot, https://kahoot.it)

3. Flipped lessons (Khan Academy, https://khanacademy.org; YouTube, https://youtube.com; and TED-Ed, https://ed.ted.com)

4. Blogging sites for students (Weebly, https://weebly.com; Wix, https://wix.com; and WordPress, https://wordpress.com)

5. Cloud storage (Google Drive, https://google.com/drive; Microsoft OneDrive, https://onedrive.live.com/about; and Dropbox, www.dropbox.com)

6. Gamification (Minecraft, https://minecraft.net/en-us; Classcraft, https://classcraft.com; and Gamestar Mechanic, https://gamestarmechanic.com)

Technology will always be a part of students' lives and of their learning, but it need not be something educators fear or revile. After all, the greatest piece of technology we'll ever have in our classrooms is a teacher with a passion for learning. However, by using edtech tools like these, you can provide students with modes of learning that connect with a digital world they are already familiar with, creating more relevance for them.

Reflection

After you complete this activity with your students, take some time to reflect on and answer the following questions.

- How much more engaged are students when you allow them to use personal technology and social networks to assist their learning?

- How else can learning continue to happen both inside and outside school when students are using familiar technologies?

Use Student-Designed Assignments

Often, one of the most effective ways to ensure connection and relevance for learners is to employ a personalized learning method whereby students design the assignments themselves. We delve more fully into this kind of shift in chapter 3 (page 35), but it's important to get that ball rolling here because when learners have a say in how teachers design their lessons, the personal connection is almost instantaneous and the stake they have in their learning is considerably higher. They gain a more emotional investment and a better attachment to the learning outcomes once they have a full understanding of the criteria you are assessing them on, since they personally have helped set them. Seek student input on your next lesson design, and work with your learners as a class to agree on projects, assessment criteria, timelines, milestones, ongoing assessment activities, and more.

Activity

Students learn best when they are interested, inquisitive, or inspired. Consequently, student learning and performance can potentially suffer when students are bored or disengaged. Concepts, mandated curriculum, and state standards may be set in your school, and you may feel like your hands are tied sometimes; nevertheless, you can still influence the delivery of the material and provide lessons that speak to your learners' interests and learning styles. Here are four ideas to involve students in the design process for your upcoming lessons.

1. **Allow students guided options in how they would like to learn the material:** Give them more say in choosing a topic to investigate and write about. For example, let them collaborate on Pinterest boards to organize, comment, and share materials.

2. **Let them choose how to demonstrate what they learn:** Multimedia presentations, such as using audio and video applications, can help with engaging students through their creativity. Let them demonstrate concepts by tying technology in the classroom to content and lessons in ways that are relevant and interesting to them.

3. **Let them self- and peer assess:** Self- and peer-assessment support comes from both students and teachers. Encouraging reflection and self-assessment can be a powerful dimension to learning because I have found it fosters a sense of personal responsibility in students for their learning. In addition, it reduces a teacher's workload and lets students effectively demonstrate understanding. Students are honest in their assessment of their performance and that of their peers and value each other's insights because it helps them understand the process of their own learning. It also reinforces the importance of collaboration. I write more about self- and peer assessment in chapter 10 (page 121).

4. **Let them teach for a week:** Assign each student a week where he or she gets to act as the teacher for a set amount of time on a concept or idea of his or her choice. Students' teaching time doesn't have to be very long, maybe fifteen minutes per day for a week. Because they will need time to plan their lessons in advance and prepare for their teaching week, get them involved well in advance so they can effectively explore an idea or concept. You can prepare them for each day's lesson beforehand in perhaps an hour or even less, but you'll have to gauge how much time it will take to prepare them for multiple days in advance. Use your best judgment and be on hand to offer them insights on how best to conduct their instruction.

Using strategies like these to personalize learning engages students' creativity and gives them broader context and relevance for learning topics.

Reflection

After you complete this activity with your students, take some time to reflect on and answer the following questions.

- How much deeper was your learners' connection to the lesson when they had input in creating it?

- How did the outcomes change?

- What was their most meaningful discovery when designing their own learning?

Summary

Teachers and students are both human, and humans are emotional beings. Indeed, learning itself is an emotionally charged experience. Think back to a time when you were young and had an aha moment in one of your own classroom learning experiences. How did you feel when you realized you finally had a complete understanding of a concept? Did you feel joy, elation, and a personal sense of accomplishment? How did the adventure of learning and discovery feel to you then? It's through this emotional conduit that learning resonates with us and becomes meaningful, and the same is true for the learners in our classrooms. It's those moments we strive to provide for them as teachers.

The type of learning that sparks emotion and connection by association and relevance is far and away the most powerful learning we can experience, both as teachers and as students. Because as a teacher your learning never ends, you are in a prime position to positively model a mindset of being a lifelong learner to every student you encounter. The more we connect students with learning at a contextual level that is relevant to their lives, the more we transform learning into a deeply personal experience. Your students can experience some of that through the microshifts in this chapter, but the next shift (the next step) is to truly embrace personalized learning even beyond what we explored here.

Guiding Questions

As you reflect on this chapter, consider the following five guiding questions.

1. Why are connection and relevance so vital to successful learning?

2. How do emotional connections fit into the learning process?

3. What kinds of heartfelt questions can you ask students to emotionally engage them in the learning for your curriculum?

4. In what ways can you use edtech to connect students with learning topics?

5. What else can you do beyond the microshifts in this chapter to make learning relevant to your learners?

Personalized Learning

Traditional instructional practices often dismiss personalizing learning for each student. I've seen education stakeholders across the spectrum claim it's too challenging and time consuming to apply to large groups of students, and it requires real effort from educators to succeed. These challenges are surmountable, and it's important that we do surmount them, because personalized learning is also a critical component of effective instruction that gets students invested in their own success.

Imagine you are going to an eye doctor because you are having trouble with your vision. You make the appointment, arrive and prepare yourself mentally, and enter the examination room. The doctor performs your eye exam, determines you need corrective lenses, and writes a prescription for you; the problem is solved, or so you believe. Now, imagine that when your glasses finally arrive, you put them on only to find, to your dismay, that your vision is worse than before. You return to the eye doctor and explain what happened and that there must be a mistake with your prescription. "Not at all," the doctor replies. "That's the same prescription for my own eyeglasses. It works for me, so there's no reason why it shouldn't work for you."

Can you imagine ever again having faith in the qualifications of this doctor? Of course not, which is why no eye doctor would do this in real life. All good medical professionals realize that not all patients have the exact same ailments, nor do they always require identical forms of treatment. Doctors individualize, differentiate, and personalize their approach according to the needs of each particular patient in order to obtain the most positive results for the vast number of people they treat. So it is with educators working with complex and versatile learners.

I often see educators confuse personalized learning with differentiation when there is, in fact, a significant difference between them. Differentiation usually involves all learners doing the same teacher-prescribed task regardless of their having any connection to it; the educator simply scales the task for each student's capacity. Personalization is different. It is the process of creating an individual pathway through learning to arrive at the required outcomes in a way that is relevant to each learner.

This third shift of practice, personalizing learning, happens when educators use connections that are relevant to learners' interest between the task and the individual student to strengthen his or her learning. As I wrote in the previous chapter, consider if there is an emotional connection to each of your learners, and if not, how might you create one?

As teachers, we accomplish this by taking advantage of focusing on topics and matters of importance to our students and finding ways to correlate them directly to our curriculum, pedagogy, and the learning environment itself. Educators can also personalize learning by taking advantage of the endless possibilities that appear in front of us every day for creating informal learning opportunities, or *teachable moments*. These are unplanned or unscheduled incidents or situations that allow an educator to provide practical insight or wisdom to learners. For example, think of an educator teaching a lesson on technological dependency in society, and suddenly, the power goes out. This is an immediate and unforeseeable opportunity for this educator to encourage students to adapt their learning to a real-life situation right in front of them. When you can locate these moments, we help our students attain a better understanding of a lesson.

Learning is a personal experience because it is something we do ourselves. No one can learn for us. The practice of personalizing learning is all about tailoring tasks and instruction to the expansive range of interests and learning styles that characterize modern learners and doing so in creative and engaging ways. Traditional 20th century education in industrialized nations fostered a whole-group instructional approach because the primary purpose of the school system was to create industrial workers (Jukes, McCain, & Crockett, 2010). Consequently, many of these students would graduate to factory roles and perform the same tasks day in and day out for much of their lives. This is not a model built for the needs of 21st century students who are entering a world that demands creative, analytical, and problem-solving skills (Crockett, 2016b). In this world, all teachers must be able to differentiate their instruction to some degree to effect better outcomes for students and prepare them for professional life in the 21st century.

I believe that if a teacher does the teaching in a classroom, then we must consider that he or she is most likely teaching just one student. If other students happen to be similar, are willing to be passively compliant, or are emotionally engaged, they will also benefit. But what about the rest of the learners? Education systems trim the top and bottom ends of classes, labeling some as learning challenged and in need of special education with more strict and explicit instruction. Others get the designation of gifted and talented and receive unique opportunities for deeper and more personal engagement. It's ironic and unfortunate, considering what we discuss in chapter 2 (page 21) about relevance and engagement, that we create more learning opportunities for learners who are accelerating and even less for learners who are struggling.

As it pertains to personalized learning, it's also important to understand that modern digital learners are different from their counterparts in previous generations (Crockett, 2016b). No longer are we catering to one specific type of learner destined for a limited array of occupations or societal roles once they leave their school experiences behind. Digital learners are unique, challenging, and rewarding to have as students because constant digital exposure during formative years digitally enhances and completely rewires them to expect instantaneous and rewarding learning that happens *just in time* instead of *just in case*. For example, they don't require knowledge *just in case* they want to become scientists, mathematicians, or historians, but rather they need knowledge that is *just in time* to give them what they need to continue to do what they are doing in the moment, a moment that may require scientific, mathematical, or historical knowledge. To facilitate rather than inhibit their success, we must nurture them as problem solvers, independent thinkers, and entrepreneurs. These young minds we cultivate must be ready to take on multidisciplinary vocations we've not yet invented and solve problems we can't even conceive.

In this chapter, I examine the characteristics of personalized learning and then delve into three microshifts of practice you can use in your own classroom to engage students at an individual level.

The Characteristics of Personalized Learning

The rapid pace of technological development around the world requires that every citizen be a lifelong learner (Demirel, 2009). For this reason, the idea of being in school tends to tag along with students even after classes are over and done. Facing the challenges this world presents means students need to have strong problem-solving skills, an ability to adapt to shifting workplace cultures, a capacity for critical and independent thinking, and certainly the skills to continue learning and growing throughout their lives (Crockett, 2016b). Imparting to students these invaluable gifts for living well can come through shifting into the practice of personalizing learning. When we personalize learning for students, we help them develop a passion for it by showing them that it can be interesting if we're willing to make it interesting to them.

Let's begin our exploration of how teachers can personalize learning by looking at some of the characteristics that define it. Personalized learning:

- Tailors instruction to the learner's interests and capabilities in a way that connects to curriculum

- Offers relevant tasks that encourage a shift of responsibility for learning to the learner

- Paces itself to accommodate every student's learning speed and style

- Incorporates technology to successfully connect to learners' interests
- Utilizes formative assessments that can include both self-conducted and peer-conducted methods
- Allows students to take a certain amount of control over what they learn and how they learn it

In addition to these, it's worth mentioning that all shifts of practice, including personalized learning, retain the goal of cultivating skills that are essential to a successful life beyond school. The modern-life skills students need are much different from the ones students raised in the 20th century required before the technological revolution swept the world. Personalized learning gives all students a chance to obtain these skills by shifting the responsibility for learning to them in comfortable learner-centered surroundings that allow them to progress at their own pace.

When you consider personalizing learning, it seems like a lofty notion to take on. After all, teachers naturally measure the viability of such a concept against the hard reality that there can be dozens of students in one classroom, and hundreds—even thousands—in a single school. How can we possibly expect to accommodate the individual needs of each student with a personalized instructional program? What does it take to truly personalize learning in modern classrooms?

As with any big shift, you can make personalized learning a reality by applying careful planning and a system of ongoing evaluation and refinement. I elaborate on this point later in this chapter, but it's important to understand that, thanks to technology, learners already do much of this work on their own. Consider how students incorporate various media formats into engineering their own personal projects and pursuits. They are so comfortable and familiar with technology that they couldn't imagine being able to learn without it. It's not much of a stretch to channel that enthusiasm into the classroom.

Another thing to consider is that you don't have to personalize every activity and progression in the learning challenge. There is value for learners in having the grit to do something that they may not want to do. It is a question of constant balance because, without sufficient personalization, a learner will disconnect and potentially disengage completely. Where this point is varies learner by learner, which is why, as we stated in *Mindful Assessment* (Crockett & Churches, 2017), "We should not see learning as the outcome of teaching but rather allow teaching to become a mindful response to learning" (p. 2).

Personalized instruction requires a versatile approach to learning in which your responses to learner variance can take many forms. It isn't necessary to tailor every single progression or activity of the learning challenge to each individual learner. The conversation around the essential question represents a tremendous opportunity to uncover clues to personalization. During this discussion, it will be clear which aspects or tangents appeal to which learners. Think back to the essential-question content on discussing health and illness with students (page 10). This is an example of how many such interactions could happen.

Beyond using the discussion that ensues after asking an essential question, you can personalize your instruction by focusing on the following.

- **Task:** Tailor tasks to specific learners' needs and interests.

- **Learning process:** Identify the steps learners take in getting from one concept to the next. All students learn at different speeds and sometimes take different pathways to discovery.

- **Research:** Understand how learners prefer to conduct research using either traditional or digital sources.

- **Evidence of learning created:** Allow for how each learner chooses to demonstrate understanding through what he or she creates as a product or as a solution.

- **Role in collaboration:** Recognize what each student brings to the collaborative environment in terms of communication, participation, and personal skills.

Note that you can and should combine all these options. When personalizing instruction, you can also incorporate components from flipped learning or blended learning practice. Think of flipped learning as a reversal of traditional classroom instruction in which you provide recorded instruction (usually in the form of videos) for students to view and internalize outside of school, while using classroom time to have students work on practical applications of that instruction. The video instruction aspect of flipped learning allows the learner to learn at his or her own pace and in comfortable surroundings outside of school. In addition, on-demand flipped learning materials make content available to those who struggle slightly more to absorb learning to review it as much as they need to.

Blended learning is a style of instruction that incorporates online learning outside the school with learning inside the physical school building as part of an integrated learning experience (Maxwell, 2016). By taking advantage of students' access to learning materials wherever they are and at any time, teachers make learning a much more personal experience.

Microshifts of Practice: Learning Is Personal

Making learning more personal for students is something all teachers can do, no matter the size of their class or the subject they teach. In this section, I describe three methods: (1) create diverse learning areas, (2) use reflective questioning, and (3) conduct interviews or surveys. Each section includes a specific activity you can use with students and reflective questions you can ask yourself about how your students responded.

Create Diverse Learning Areas

Personalized learning can only work if you organize your classroom to facilitate it. When I visit a school, the typical classroom I see is set up for factory-style learning with desks in traditional rows. Instead, organize your classroom to accommodate different learning areas. For example, a better floor plan may involve one station for students conducting research on laptops, another with some comfortable couch seating and a whiteboard or SMART Board for small-group instruction, and one area for viewing videos or working on multimedia projects. For your next lesson, try dividing your classroom into different learning areas (start with no more than three) using these kinds of stations or something similar. Try getting input from your students on how best to arrange desks into patterns that promote a collaborative atmosphere, and what each section can be for.

Activity

To get started reorganizing your class for personalized learning, understand that your learners need an environment that they can connect with and be inspired by. No matter what your learning areas will ultimately be, they should be welcoming and as spacious as possible, so make efficient use of your available space or take advantage of other room options around your school. You'll need space if your learning areas incorporate movement of any kind.

Maybe you're going for more traditional setups using chairs, benches, and workstations. Maybe you're making creative use of couches and cushions so that students can get creative and collaborate more comfortably. In either case, don't forget about decorating. Include art, plants, colors, music, and examples of the kinds of work that you and your students are inspiring each other to accomplish.

The next thing to determine is the type of work that will go on in each area. You'll likely have learning areas devoted to specific actions as part of the learning process. These might include the following types of areas.

- **Research and reading:** A section with computers and more traditional sources of information that are specifically for conducting research

- **Collaborative discussion:** A section based on making interaction with each other easy, in which you should ensure you provide a setup that allows learners to face each other, make eye contact, and understand each other clearly

- **Multimedia interactivity:** A section with audio and video stations for listening and viewing; also includes equipment and tools for creating such projects

- **Building and construction:** A section with workshop-style areas for building and experimenting with hands-on projects or makerspaces

- **Lab work and testing:** A section for scientific or laboratory-style creation and experimentation, especially in a STEM classroom

All of these learning areas are based on providing learners with the things they love most—connection, collaboration, and creation. Such provisions extend beyond the basic processes of sitting at desks and memorizing content and enter into learning realms that exercise the higher end of Bloom's taxonomy (Anderson & Krathwohl, 2001). Additionally, they get learners up and moving around, experiencing different avenues of learning, and connecting with friends and peers, all of which can make learning considerably more enjoyable and more effective for them.

Reflection

After you complete this activity with your students, take some time to reflect on and answer the following questions.

- How did the student groups use each learning section?

- Were there smooth transitions from area to area?

- What differences did you notice, if any, in your learners' productivity or concentration levels?

- Was the change in the environment an overall positive or negative experience for the class? Would you do it again? If so, what would you change or include?

Use Reflective Questioning

The power of *reflective questioning*—questions that ask students to contemplate what they've learned or experienced—to connect learners to the instruction they receive presents a powerful way to personalize learning and is worthy of regular practice in your classroom. At any time during the learning process, teachers should always ask questions that allow learners to reflect on and debrief their processes in highly personal ways (Crockett, 2017a). You can't just ask any questions, however. It's easy enough to ask students questions when something makes sense to them or if they understand a concept. Such questions won't always receive entirely truthful responses in the first place because, regardless of what they personally think, students will answer with what they know to be the "correct" reply.

It's much better to ask students the type of reflective questions that help them connect with learning on an emotional level. Ask them what about their learning resonated with them and where they experienced a disconnect. Urge them to consider what they could change or improve to make better use of their class time. Get them curious to talk with you and with each other about what they still question and what they want to learn.

This kind of reflective discussion is what the debrief phase of solution fluency is all about (see page 79). It's a phase that educators often overlook, but it's an entirely essential part of the process that guides students to take a good look at the day's learning and judge how effective it was for them, where it was most powerful, and what could change to offer them a stronger emotional and intellectual connection.

As I discuss in the following activity, for educators it's all in asking the right reflective questions. Ideally, this is something you do at the end of the lesson, when all projects are complete, presented, and assessed. It needn't take any longer than the time it takes to let everyone have their say and share their insights in a brief and concise manner. You may also have to set time aside for lengthier discussions at your own discretion and depending on what learners feel is necessary.

Activity

The following lists some examples of the kinds of questions you can ask during end-of-class reflection discussions.

- What worked best today and what didn't work?
- How could you improve on what you've done?
- What are three things you learned today that you didn't know before?
- What are two things that surprised you?
- What one thing do you still want to learn?
- What was your most inspiring moment today?
- What was your most difficult moment?
- How can you apply what you've learned to other challenges now and in the future?

The next step is to analyze how students responded to the questions. You can use all questions in this manner either as an open dialogue with learners or as an exit ticket they can write about for the final ten minutes of class and submit before they leave for the day.

Reflection

After you complete this activity with your students, take some time to reflect on and answer the following questions.

- How did students respond to the questions you asked? Were they more open to sharing their insights and feelings than you thought, or less? Why do you think that is? If successful, is this a practice you'd be willing to recommend to colleagues?

- How do you think this kind of questioning can be beneficial for both you and your learners?

Conduct Interviews or Surveys

Part of successfully personalizing learning is finding out where your students are in terms of their own academic expectations, which helps you determine where they want or need to be and plan how to get them there. Informal interviews or quick surveys can be useful tools in making these initial assessments. It doesn't have to be a time-consuming process, but thoughtful questions will help you discover what you can about the diverse assumptions and learning styles of the students you'll be going on the journey with.

The humble survey is one of the best tools we have for collecting data to help customize a wide range of products and services. Interviews and questionnaires, both of which you can use to quickly gather a large amount of relevant data, are probably the most common delivery methods for surveys. From there, evaluating and analyzing the data can provide you with insights into how you can best develop a project that caters to the needs and preferences of your students.

Activity

You can supplement or replace face-to-face student interviews by designing online surveys that they complete outside of school and providing links. To do this, explore online tools like SurveyMonkey (https://surveymonkey.com), Google Forms (https://google.com/forms/about), Survey Planet (https://surveyplanet.com), and others, each of which make it possible to create and distribute engaging survey questions.

Whether you use an interview or online survey, I suggest you pose three different questions that will provide you with a general sense of where students are in their learning and what they expect from you before you embark on a new topic. Here are some examples.

- How do you feel right now about what we are covering in class?

- Do you have any questions about the lesson or lessons that are most important to you right now?

- What are you hoping to learn about in the topics we will cover?

As educators, we want to make sure we inspire deep thinking in our students about their learning journeys. Other examples of questions can pertain to things like how what they've learned has changed their idea of learning in general, how they can apply new knowledge to other problems, and what its significance is in the real world.

Reflection

After you complete this activity with your students, take some time to reflect on and answer the following questions.

- What was your overall impression of the learners' responses? How did they differ from your expectations?

- Were there any responses that surprised you or that you didn't expect?

- What did you learn about your students and their expectations for learning?

- How can you and your learners work together to meet or exceed each other's expectations in the best way possible?

Summary

Personalized learning is learning that strives to meet each of our students as they are—diverse and unique, aware and inquisitive, and complex yet understandable. By incorporating the flexibility of personalization into our instructional approach with careful balance and a strong commitment to fostering lifelong learning skills in all learners regardless of style or capability, we well prepare them to confidently embrace future challenges no matter what they move on to after they graduate. This confidence also allows each learner to take on the kinds of higher-order-thinking tasks I discuss in the next chapter.

Guiding Questions

As you reflect on this chapter, consider the following five guiding questions.

1. What is personalized learning, and why is it important in modern education?

2. Why do you think some educators find personalizing learning difficult to implement or often don't have much success with it?

3. What role can personalized learning play in fostering lifelong learning?

4. How might you use diverse learning areas to facilitate more individualized learning for your students and how might doing so make for more effective learning?

5. How might you use reflective questions and interview or survey questions to better develop personalized learning practices with your own learners?

chapter 4

A Challenge of Higher-Order-Thinking Skills

There is a global migration of curricula taking place that affects everything from learning content to instructional processes, and it's driving a focus on critical and creative thinking. From Australia's General Capabilities (Australian Curriculum, Assessment and Reporting Authority, n.d.) to New Zealand's Key Competencies (New Zealand Ministry of Education, n.d.), from the International Baccalaureate (n.d.b) program's learner profiles to the Common Core (National Governors Association Center for Best Practices & Council of Chief State School Officers, n.d.), critical, creative, and analytical thinking top the list of priorities education experts highlight for learners.

Relative to traditional 20th century education practices, these standards require a dramatic transformation in pedagogy, but as I highlighted at the start of this book, whatever pedagogy your school adopts, you can use the essential shifts in this book to improve learning and learner engagement in your classroom.

Higher-order-thinking skills, like creative and analytical thinking, are not content-recall skills. Simply put, there is no way for teachers to test prep students for thinking. It is something we must cultivate through our daily instructional practices. Because of this, a remarkable shift is taking place. Disappearing is the focus on educational bulimia (the memorization and regurgitation of content), and in its place schools are increasingly focusing attention on tasks that require the higher end of Bloom's taxonomy—the skills of analyzing, evaluating, and creating (Anderson & Krathwohl, 2001).

This is evident in schools such as Melrose High School in Pearce, Australia. At Melrose, years 9 and 10 learners spend their time connecting to learning through valuable experiences such as working on community projects, taking on school leadership roles, mentoring younger students, writing thesis-based work and building portfolios, and participating in various exhibitions that highlight their learning careers and accomplishments (S. Vaughan, personal communication, 2017). Every one of these requires learners to engage in challenging higher-order-thinking skills and be creative.

By encouraging learners to evaluate and create on a consistent basis, we connect with many of the other shifts in this book, including personalization (chapter 3, page 35), process-oriented learning (chapter 6, page 75), and learner creation (chapter 8, page 101).

In this chapter, I write about the benefits of challenging students to embrace their creativity and engaging them in tasks that require them to use higher-order-thinking skills. To begin, I establish the importance of student engagement in this process—specifically, the importance of ensuring students display awareness of and connection to their learning tasks. From there, I provide three microshifts of practice you can use in your own classroom to challenge students in ways that stir and develop their higher-order-thinking skills.

The Road to Awareness and Connection

Challenging students to engage their higher-order-thinking skills requires that you have and maintain their engagement in the tasks you assign. In chapter 2 (page 21), I write about the fact that students' engagement with their own learning increases when instruction provides them with increased context and relevance. With no connection there can be no interest, and interest is what always precedes meaningful learning that sticks. Likewise, in *Mindful Assessment* (Crockett & Churches, 2017), Andrew Churches and I introduce the assessment framework for the essential fluencies. To the bottom of Bloom's revised taxonomy (Anderson & Krathwohl, 2001), we added the elements of awareness and connection. Awareness is obviously necessary for learning to occur because we can't remember something of which we are not even aware. Connection is also critical to learning because without it learning does not occur—thus, our insistence on constantly striving to create strong emotional connections to the learning. In respect to critical thinking, the importance of connecting to learning warrants revisiting. In this section, we establish connections to learning through awareness, evaluation, and creation. We follow this up with a look at the needs of the professional world and how these practices better prepare students to find success in it.

The Importance of Connection to Learning

The line that separates teaching from learning is between connection and remembering, so the teacher's role is to bring learning concepts within the grasp of students by taking advantage of a strong connection as we discussed in chapter 2, and providing the opportunity to access new knowledge and develop new skills. The learning is up to the students.

Once entering our consciousness through awareness, connection becomes the critical factor that determines which of Bloom's revised taxonomy levels the learning has the potential to reach (Anderson & Krathwohl, 2001). When we don't challenge students, they don't connect with content, and their learning doesn't rise above the lower end of Bloom's revised taxonomy. This may be enough for students to pass the course, but once they've done so, they will simply dispense with the knowledge because they have no need for it anymore. With a high level of emotional connection, which you reach by providing tasks that promote higher-order thinking, you can drive the learning all the way to the level of creating rather than letting it rest at remembering, understanding, and (possibly) applying learned knowledge. By perceiving high personal relevance, students place increased value on the knowledge they acquire and take on ownership of it. When learners own their learning, they own it forever.

Evaluation and Creation Skills in the Professional World

Challenging our students to evaluate and create makes them effective *prosumers of knowledge*, meaning they both consume and produce the knowledge. The importance of being a prosumer of knowledge has much to do with how industry and business in the digital age have shifted (Crockett et al., 2011). It made sense for communities to configure Industrial Revolution–era schools to develop students into factory workers tasked with generally lower-order-thinking jobs. That is no longer a reality. In modern business, what gives any organization the edge in a global market saturated with limitless opportunities for locking in consumer loyalty is how workers design a product. As we stated in our book *Literacy Is NOT Enough* (Crockett et al., 2011), "Creativity is the currency of the 21st century" (p. 44). Let's look at a couple of real-world examples.

In 2001, General Motors hired a man named Robert Lutz to help breathe some new life into the struggling company. Lutz was a former marine and a seasoned businessman who already had a previous stint at General Motors in 1963 before moving on to work for BMW, Ford, and Chrysler ("Bob Lutz [Businessman]," n.d.). When *The New York Times* asked how his approach would differ from that of his predecessors, Lutz told them, "It's more right-brained. . . . I see us in the art business. Art, entertainment, and mobile sculpture that coincidentally happens to provide transportation" (Rae-Dupree, 2008).

Another example of the importance of having creative minds for successful businesses comes from Norio Ohga, the former chairman of Sony Corporation. In the book *A Whole New Mind*, Daniel Pink (2006) quotes him in 2003: "At Sony, we assume that all products of our competitors have basically the same technology, price, performance, and features. Design is the only thing that differentiates one product from another in the marketplace" (p. 78).

Although creativity and logic are not diametrically opposed products of a hemispheric brain (Nielsen, Zielinski, Ferguson, Lainhart, & Anderson, 2013), what these gentlemen were indirectly prepping us for was the need to shift away from the traditional 20th century focus on lower-order thinking, and move toward a newer, holistic focus on the features and performance of the kind of design innovation that incorporates creativity at every level of product development.

This is one of the many reasons why I believe it is critical for teachers to focus more on adapting their instruction to involve projects that stimulate and develop students' higher-order-thinking skills. To that end, I interview thousands of educators in my travels all over the globe every year, and I always ask them what they believe are the most crucial skills learners can possess in preparation for leading successful lives outside school. Far and away, the two most consistent responses I hear are that students must have proficiency in the skills of creativity and problem solving. The challenge for teachers lies in determining the most effective way to assess these skills.

Assessment of Higher-Order-Thinking Skills

When Andrew Churches and I (2017) wrote *Mindful Assessment*, we did so in part to answer the question we have been asked in several countries as to how to assess higher-order-thinking skills. Since we published this book, there have been several interesting developments. Firstly, British Columbia (n.d.) released a new curriculum, the purpose of which is to focus on a series of core competencies. Although these are largely the same broad ideas that we have seen in other curricula initiatives, like those we cited at the start of this chapter, what is interesting to note is that they provide only a skeleton of content ideas. They act as suggestions for how one might develop a particular competency. In its new curriculum, British Columbia (n.d.) makes it clear that it will evaluate and report against the competency and not the content. I have also had ongoing, private conversations with education representatives from three states in Australia about their intent to assess and report on the General Capabilities (Australian Curriculum, Assessment and Reporting Authority, n.d.). As curricula shift to skills from knowledge, accountability structures will shift to evaluate the skills instead of content. Again, this is not as apparent in the United States as in most other countries, but I am convinced that educators around the globe will see a systemwide focus on the assessment and reporting of skills such as these.

It takes time to change the direction of a school and even a classroom as they move more like a steamship, not a fleet of kayaks, which makes it all the more imperative for schools and educators to move classroom instruction in this direction ahead of this inevitability. Schools, specifically, need to shift to future-focused, learner-centered learning, as it is the only way to cultivate these skills.

To give you one more idea of how product design changes along with costs and skill sets, we need look no further than comparing the cell phone expenditures of Motorola and Apple (Dedrick & Kraemer, 2017). In 1993, 83 percent of Motorola's cell phone production budget went to fixed costs related to manufacturing, with only 17 percent invested in research and design. In 2013, after years of success with its iPhone, Apple devoted only 13 percent of its cell phone budget to manufacturing costs, with 87 percent invested in design, marketing, distribution, and prototyping research for the next design. This is a complete reversal of the Motorola phone from 1993. The significance of this contrast goes even deeper when you consider that Apple devotes only 1 percent of its budget to the low-cognitive task of assembling its phones. The rest goes to applications that require higher-order-thinking skills that emphasize creative, persuasive, investigative, and collaborative skill sets. Not only is this the skill set in which industry is investing, it mirrors the overarching goals of the global shift in curricula many countries are undergoing.

By examining a simple product comparison, like that of Motorola and Apple, we can see how much things have changed and will continue to change. Any school that wants to prepare its students for success in the professional world must arm them with the future-focused, higher-order-thinking skills found at the top end of Bloom's revised taxonomy (Anderson & Krathwohl, 2001). On a personal note, seeing learning rich in such tasks is a joy and a privilege—learners thrive at their very best, striving together to evaluate and create solutions for problems that matter to us all.

Let's examine some microshifts of practice you can use in your own classroom to make this a reality.

Microshifts of Practice: Challenging Tasks Develop Higher-Order-Thinking Skills

Challenging students to engage and develop their higher-order-thinking skills requires everyday practice in your classroom. In this section, I describe three methods: (1) provide question periods, (2) set up a classroom blog, and (3) establish citizenship days. Each section includes a specific activity you can use with students and reflective questions you can ask yourself about how your students responded.

Provide Question Periods

A classroom is a place of discovery and exploration, where learners can feel safe asking questions that drive their learning. Note that these are different from the essential questions we talk about in chapter 1 (page 9), since they are narrower in focus and can be slightly more technical in nature, as you'll see in the activity examples that follow.

Often as educators, we use questions for recalling content and facts, but this doesn't speak to our students' higher-order-thinking abilities. Using questions that drive students' curiosity and encourage them to ask questions of their own creates opportunities to evaluate, analyze, synthesize, and apply knowledge in order to obtain the answers they seek, often going even beyond those answers and entering into new learning territory. In this way, students can internalize their learning in the best way possible.

Activity

Challenge students often during the learning process with higher-order-thinking questions that can help you assess where they are and help them discover how far they've come. Begin with three higher-order-thinking challenge questions per lesson and increase from there. Some examples of such questions include the following.

- What criteria would you use to assess _____?
- How would you determine _____?
- How would you verify _____?
- What information would you use to _____?
- What data did you use to evaluate _____?
- How would you create a plan to _____?
- What facts can you gather to _____?
- What would be a suitable alternative for _____?

You can use these questions in an open discussion to attain a general picture of where learners are at if you want to keep it simple. However, if you want to monitor responses more closely you can have them provide short or long answers in a worksheet-style activity for later review.

Reflection

After you complete this activity with your students, take some time to reflect on and answer the following questions.

- How did students respond to these exploratory questions?
- What did they discover about themselves and about each other through asking deeper questions?
- How does this information help you personally understand how to design future tasks for your learners?

Set Up a Classroom Blog

Blogging is a terrific educational practice for your learners. It's a gathering place outside of class students can use to write about ideas they've researched and then comment on each other's writing in a free-flowing environment for sharing and exchanging relevant information. Blogging develops crucial writing and communication skills and provides an excellent peer-to-peer contact platform. Because the best blogging entries entail writing well-thought-out and researched thoughts on a topic, students who engage in blogging activities build research and organizational skills while exploring topics they feel passionate about. If you haven't started a classroom blog yet, you should consider it. Here are a few other reasons why classroom blogging is good for learning in general.

- Blogging is a great learning tool for receiving feedback that helps improve learners' communication skills through writing more clearly and more accessibly to a wide range of readers.

- Blogging creates an opportunity for teaching digital citizenship by demonstrating how to be respectful to others by way of what topics students choose and how they choose to write about them.

- Blogging is good for building a student-teacher community when everyone participates in discussing great ideas for blogging topics to share with an audience.

- Blogging attracts personal learning network opportunities for teachers who want to use writing to reach out to colleagues and other educators interested in the same professional ideas and topics.

Once you're ready to set up a classroom blog, you should look for the platform that suits your needs and the needs of your students. Platforms you can consider include Blogger (https://blogger.com/about), CampusPress (https://campuspress.com), Edublogs (https://edublogs.org), Kidblog (https://kidblog.org/home), Weebly (https://weebly.com), and WordPress (https://wordpress.com). Set up an account on one of these platforms and use the tools it provides to let your students set up their own accounts and log in to the platform. Make sure to pay attention to each platform's age restrictions. (Some platforms require users to be age thirteen or older to set up an account.)

Activity

Begin this activity by discussing as a class what topics the students would like to blog about, what they know about the craft of blogging, and what blogging entails. Next, you can explain the blog's registration and log-in process (if it requires one), draft a class agreement stating guidelines and rules for maintaining the blog, and define some goals you'd like to achieve with it.

You can have students write blog content or comment on it at any time, but make sure there is classroom time for this activity if you have students who do not have internet service at home. Another consideration is how often you or your students should be blogging. At the very least a teacher should blog every week. Try to cover topics that can appeal to other educators, like professional learning interests, lesson ideas, or classroom management tips.

For students, you can set guidelines for writing their own blog entries and provide the opportunity for them to contribute as many extra entries in their free time as they want. To foster participation, require all students to contribute a comment on your entries or those of their peers. Commenting is a good exercise for students to demonstrate how well they understood the writing and what its central focus was, as well as practice being polite and respectful and constructive when giving feedback.

You may face some obstacles, such as some learners' inability to type well. Some are also less connected than others, and still other students may lack good writing skills. These can be great opportunities for enhancing instruction and challenging students to think harder on their topics or comments.

Reflection

After you complete this activity with your students, take some time to reflect on and answer the following questions.

- What are the most rewarding aspects of blogging that students have experienced?
- What were their biggest challenges?
- How are they planning to use this platform to share information and opinions?
- How are they refining their blogging techniques and what are they learning along the way?
- What unique skills do they feel blogging has helped them develop?

Establish Citizenship Days

As part of a global digital society, we are responsible for showing others the importance of treating each other and ourselves with respect and dignity in both our physical and digital environments. There is a prime opportunity in your classroom to show learners how they can work together in creating an awareness of how to treat others with decency in the online world, and in ways that are fun and entertaining. To facilitate this learning, you can have students create their own unique class participation games that teach people about digital citizenship and invite other students and teachers (and even parents) to play and learn about digital citizenship in a class activity day.

What makes this a higher-order challenge, beyond the aspect of creation, is the fact that learners must deeply consider the inner workings of the games they create and how they will work toward their games having a purpose and challenge that will actually teach the player something valuable.

Activity

To begin, have student groups research what digital citizenship is and why it's so important. There are many different web resources geared toward digital citizenship for students of all ages. They can try sites like our own Global Digital Citizen Foundation (www.globaldigitalcitizen.org), Common Sense Media (www.commonsensemedia .org), CyberWise (www.cyberwise.org), or NetSmartz (www.netsmartz.org). As students explore these and other online resources, encourage them to pay careful attention to how the resources' creators composed their work. Because these sites are all about digital citizenship, the people who write for them are generally excellent at exemplifying how to compose and present online content in a responsible way. After their research is done, conduct a follow-up discussion about what they've discovered and how they feel it will assist them in their lives.

As your students increase their knowledge of digital citizenship practices, have them explore what kinds of games they can create for both their peers and younger grade levels that would also teach or demonstrate digital citizenship. The products students produce could include word games, games that use picture matching, adventure games in which every choice has a different consequence and leads to a whole new set of choices, and more. If you want to go bigger, students could collaborate to design a board game or record a game show in which contestants display their knowledge of digital citizenship.

Encourage students to think of all the different ways they could use the games they design to turn this subject into a fun learning adventure for all. Have them consider their process for creating a game. Ask them how they can use technology to enhance their designs. Have them consider using game stations or structures like cubicles or stalls. Students should consider how they can encourage other people to play and how participants will learn to play and understand the game. Will they offer a demonstration? Will they have written rules? How easy will it be for players to access the game? Regardless of the answers to these questions, students should monitor participating players to make sure everything is working as they envisioned it.

Reflection

After you complete this activity with your students, take some time to reflect on and answer the following questions.

- What did your students learn about digital citizenship and its importance in their online lives?

- Were the students surprised at either how much or how little people knew about digital citizenship?

- What kinds of higher-order-thinking skills did students feel they displayed while engaging in the activity?

- How did they feel about the task of making their own games to use as teaching tools?

Summary

Schools that are shifting their instructional focus to emphasize creative thinking, problem solving, and other future-focused, high-order skills may at last be taking center stage to help students learn and preparing them for the professional world, but we've still got a long way to go. This shouldn't discourage you—it should inspire you. You are more than up to the task of providing your students with such learning journeys regardless of the instructional pedagogy you use in the classroom. By shifting the learning focus to more deeply emphasize challenging, higher-order-thinking tasks, you and your students grow together, you stumble and trip together, and you get back up and come back stronger together.

My hope is that by using the activities in this chapter, you can see how engaging students in difficult challenges not only builds skills for success in work and school, but also fosters resilience and the ability to adapt to failure and turn it into progress. If you would like to explore other activities you can use to challenge your students in this way, you can view my Wabisabi Learning case studies (https://wabisabilearning .com/case-studies). Each one begins with connection and relevance, then a challenge of higher-order-thinking tasks; from there the creative possibilities are endless.

In the next shift, I explain how you can apply higher-order-thinking tasks to the challenge of research in an age when information expands online exponentially by the minute.

Guiding Questions

As you reflect on this chapter, consider the following five guiding questions.

1. What does *higher-order-thinking tasks* mean?

2. What important skills do higher-order-thinking tasks develop in learners?

3. How are schools adjusting pedagogy in other parts of the world to facilitate higher-order-thinking challenges?

4. Why is creativity such an important part of a business's success in the modern digital age?

5. How do providing time for question periods, setting up a classroom blog, and establishing citizenship days provide opportunities for you to engage your students in challenging tasks that encourage them to use higher-order-thinking skills?

chapter 5

Information Fluency for Research Skills

For students, it's critical to understand how to conduct research in the digital age. Let's begin this chapter with a little pop quiz. When was the last time you: Visited a library? Used a card catalog? Bought and read a newspaper? Used microfiche? Consulted an encyclopedia?

For much of the 20th century, before the internet ushered in the information age and changed everything, these tools were society's primary modes of conducting research. If you came of age in that century, try to recall how life was before the World Wide Web entered the public domain on April 30, 1993 ("World Wide Web," n.d.). Think about how you used to search for information. How much has changed since that time? Even more important, how will things continue to change, and how will those changes continue to affect the skills modern students need to conduct research and keep themselves informed?

Our instantaneous mobile access to practically anything we wish to know has transformed the way we do business, the ways in which we communicate, and how we think about and use information. It has helped us unleash our personal creativity and self-expression with abandon. It has also completely changed our traditional notions of how learning can happen. What makes this kind of learning possible is the sheer volume of global information people produce and place online. The consequence of this is that modern learners must possess a whole new set of research and analysis skills to succeed in the professional world.

To illustrate why this is so, an article from Northeastern University states that we are producing roughly 2.5 exabytes of data every day, which translates to about 530,000,000 songs; roughly 250,000,000 Libraries of Congress; or approximately 90 years of high-definition video playback—every single day (Khoso, 2016). This is an astonishing amount of data to say the least, and it's a safe bet that it won't slow down anytime soon. So the question is what all this means for learners and how it applies to preparing them for their futures.

If being an expert means possessing unique knowledge unavailable to others, then it is becoming increasingly difficult to be an expert. Simply put, if anyone in the room with you has a smartphone on him or her, you are no longer the smartest person in the room. For teachers, this is a wonderful opportunity. No longer must you shackle yourself with the responsibility of disseminating information. With ubiquitous access to information, being the person with the answers is an ineffective use of your time and capabilities! A teacher's real value is in facilitating in students a deep understanding of the meaning and application of specific information. To create lifelong, capable, and independent learners, consider that learners can access content on their own and come to us with the kinds of purposeful questions that let you personalize their learning and develop their higher-order-thinking skills. Another key component of developing information fluency in students is making sure that their learning intentions are clear, which is a topic I explore in more depth in chapter 7 (page 91).

In this chapter, you will learn more about information fluency for the purposes of research. Each of the pedagogies I spoke of in this book's introduction—STEM, STEAM, project-based learning, and inquiry—involve a component of research. Teachers and their students use information in lots of ways. Some examples include projects and assignments, professional development, and personal betterment. However, from an instructional standpoint, the information learners obtain and use for their purposes in the classroom needs to be relevant, accurate, and useful, and students must be able to quickly source it from the massive ocean of digital knowledge they have access to. Of course, this means not simply typing a question into a search engine and reading the first response, but being a discerning, active, and skeptical information consumer. This requires higher-order-thinking research skills geared toward proper acquisition and analytical techniques. We teach these skills through the application of information fluency, a concept Andrew Churches and I (2017) establish as an essential fluency in *Mindful Assessment*.

For the purposes of this chapter, I present a detailed breakdown of the structure underpinning information fluency as it applies to research. From there, I provide three microshifts of practice you can use in your own classroom to help students develop their research techniques and think critically about the information they find.

Research and the Power of Information Fluency

Information fluency is the ability to unconsciously and intuitively interpret information in all forms and formats to extract essential knowledge, perceive its meaning and significance, and use it to complete real-world tasks. There are five distinct stages to the information fluency process, which I call the *five As* (Crockett & Churches, 2017).

1. **Ask** meaningful and purposeful questions to obtain the most relevant and useful data possible. This involves fully understanding the problem, identifying key words and forming questions around them, brainstorming, thinking laterally, listening deeply, viewing wisely, speaking critically, filtering information "white noise," and sharing personal knowledge and experience.

2. **Acquire** a sufficient amount of information on the background of the research subject from plenty of traditional and digital sources. This involves determining where that information is and what skills are necessary to find it; prioritizing search strategies; skimming, scanning, and scouring all sources for pertinent data; filtering; taking smart notes; and continuing to apply the *ask* stage to the data search.

3. **Analyze** the content for relevancy and credibility, authenticate it, and arrange it all appropriately for the most efficient application possible. This stage is about organizing, triangulating, and summarizing the data; checking data for relevance and distinguishing between legitimate and untrustworthy sources; differentiating fact from opinion; assessing the currency of all information; and examining it for underlying meaning, opinion, and bias.

4. **Apply** the knowledge to use within the context of the original purpose for conducting the research. For learners, this usually involves creating some kind of a product, which could mean an essay, a report, a presentation, an experiment, or a multimedia project. Learners could also apply their newfound knowledge by participating in a debate or even just creating an argument against another point of view.

5. **Assess** the effectiveness of the knowledge application and determine if the purpose for conducting it is fulfilled. Here, students ask questions about the processes and the information they gathered and reflect critically on both. They assess what they learned and how they learned it, what worked, what didn't work, and how they could make the process and the product better the next time around. Assessing also includes making a definitive plan for acting on these reflections, internalizing new learning, and potentially transferring experiences to other situations and circumstances.

The internet is a swelling ocean of information. Navigating through the steady flow of that information ocean can be hazardous, and this is certainly true of a student who is not informationally fluent. Although it's entirely possible and acceptable to do so, students don't necessarily need to follow each step within the five As as a linear pathway to sourcing and using information. When engaging in the research component of any lesson, learners can use each stage in a cyclical process, revisiting previous stages as they gain new insights. What they create is a common language between teachers and themselves and a continuum for lifelong learning from early years to old age. As young learners utilize information fluency over a period of months or years, their capacity compounds. I have been fortunate to see this growth over a period of years with many of my clients. In the following sections, I more thoroughly examine the five As of information fluency, starting each with an essential question. You can find even more, along with a framework for assessing this skill, in *Mindful Assessment* (Crockett & Churches, 2017).

Ask

What am I looking for, and how might I best structure questions that lead to it?

For students, answering this essential question involves compiling a list of critical questions about what knowledge or data they seek. The key is to ask questions that have focus and purpose, because that's how you get the most useful answers. In my experience, well-considered exploratory questions train the mind to think critically and search for the relevant and useful data. They also help us unearth the most valuable information sources in any personal knowledge quest. When learners have a full awareness of and specific questions about what they research, they will start off on the right path.

Students must design the questions they ask to get them to certain points of discovery and realization, and that means knowing what they are looking for and why it's important to their search. When learners are unclear about their intended destination, they could end up wasting an enormous amount of the time they've devoted to researching their content. They could end up leafing through books or surfing the web and getting nowhere, or worse, they could head down the wrong information alley and get irretrievably distracted from their initial purpose.

Acquire

Where should I look, and how and whom should I ask these questions?

Accessing information is no longer a matter of going to a card catalog and getting a book or another paper-based resource. The information learners seek won't always be in one location, nor are all sources equally viable. In addition to finding a single viable source, learners must be sure to utilize as many others as possible; this includes sources that are both digital and nondigital in nature. The internet, ebooks, articles, libraries, videos, and subject matter experts all provide them with different avenues for finding information.

In this acquisition stage, it isn't necessary for learners to have read content in depth quite yet. The goal is for them to amass a solid and diverse database of knowledge that they can purposefully filter and edit in the following stages. For example, a student could take a quick cursory glance for relevancy and gather all his or her search findings into lists for later scrutiny. In that vein, learners must know how to optimize their search behaviors to obtain the best results in a reasonable time frame. Learning and using advanced search techniques is immensely helpful in speeding research.

Analyze

How do I know the information I find is useful, valid, and authentic?

After collecting raw data, the next step is to navigate through the information to authenticate, organize, and arrange it all. This stage also involves ascertaining whether information is true or not, distinguishing the good from the bad and fact from opinion, and attempting to detect where there is clear evidence of slant or bias. When it comes to online searches, some percentage of that free information is meaningless or otherwise invalid. Learners must know how to scrutinize and organize all data they collect. They should look at this stage as performing background checks on data to authenticate their validity.

For example, many search results will display similar threads (concepts) that point to repeated experiences and commonalities that appear across a broad range of sources. Some sources will share more threads than others, meaning that those sources containing fewer often-seen facts will suddenly start to take a back seat. This isn't foolproof. Sometimes a source is unique because it goes into unusual depth and insight, but comparing sources is one of the many ways the facts about what we seek can begin to reveal themselves. Students should strive to examine closely any data they collect and resources they use to source them. They should listen to and watch all videos carefully and not just skim them. They should take plenty of time to internalize what that article or webpage is trying to say, who wrote it, and why. Do they disagree or agree? Lead students toward getting a sense of how this awareness fits into their research scheme.

The *analyze* stage can easily be the area of information fluency that your learners spend most of their time in. Depending on the scope of the project or task, they can linger between the *acquiring* and *analyzing* stages, and that's a good thing. Information fluency, like all the other essential fluencies, should be a cyclical process.

Apply

How will I use what I've learned?

Once students collect and verify data and then form a solution, they must practically apply the knowledge within the context of the original purpose for the information quest. After all that hard work asking, acquiring, and analyzing, your learners have got to make that knowledge work for them. The application could be that it is the *discover* phase of solution fluency (see page 78, Solution Fluency) or that they use it to support an argument or opinion formed in reflecting on an essential question. The point is that they required that research for a purpose and have applied it to that context.

If a student's application of knowledge doesn't answer his or her question or conquer the challenge, it's time for him or her to back up a few steps. For example, the student might have required the information as background to the *dream* phase in a solution-fluency task, but upon returning to the problem, he or she finds it requires a different direction or approach. Students shouldn't be alarmed when they encounter this kind of failure—it's an opportunity to revisit a process and grow from that experience.

Assess

How can I be sure I've accomplished my research goals and how best can I improve this process?

The final stage is when students thoroughly and critically revisit both their product and the process. This involves open and lively discussions about how they could make their research journey more efficient and how they could apply the solution they created to similar challenges. This is a reflective stage in the journey in which learners look back at the steps they took to find what they were looking for. In this stage, they should also consider what the proper application of their knowledge has produced. Reflective questions for this stage can include questions like the following.

- Did we solve our problem?
- Did we answer our question?
- Did we meet our challenge?
- What did we learn?
- Was the information we found ultimately useful? Why or why not?
- What could we have done differently?
- How could we have streamlined our process and made it more efficient?
- How can we use what we've learned in other situations?

I have developed two resources that can help immensely with this process: *The Critical Thinking Skills Cheatsheet* (Crockett, 2016a) and *Use These 5 Steps to Learn How to Ask Good Questions* (Crockett, 2017b). Users have downloaded the first over 250,000 times, and some of them have translated it into other languages. It offers a range of questions around *who, what, where, when, why,* and *how.*

- **Who:** Who benefits from this? Who is this harmful to? Who makes decisions about this? Who is most directly affected? Who have you also heard discuss this? Who would be the best person to consult? Who will be the key people in this? Who deserves recognition for this?

- **What:** What are the strengths or weaknesses? What is another perspective? What is another alternative? What would be a counterargument? What are the best- and worst-case scenarios? What is most and least important? What can we do to make a positive change? What is getting in the way of our action?

- **Where:** Where would we see this in the real world? Where are there similar concepts or situations? Where is there the most need for this? Where in the world would this be a problem? Where can we get more information? Where do we go for help with this? Where will this idea take us? Where are the areas for improvement?

- **When:** When is this acceptable or unacceptable? When would this benefit our society? When would this cause a problem? When is the best time to take action? When will we know we've succeeded? When has this played a part in our history? When can we expect this to change? When should we ask for help with this?

- **Why:** Why is this a problem or challenge? Why is it relevant to me or others? Why is this the best or worst scenario? Why are people influenced by this? Why should people know about this? Why has it been this way for so long? Why have we allowed this to happen? Why is there a need for this today?

- **How:** How is this similar to _____? How does this disrupt things? How do we know the truth about this? How will we approach this safely? How does this benefit us or others? How does this harm us or others? How do we see this in the future? How can we change this for our good?

It is very useful to help students reflect critically by asking them these pointed questions. Many teachers I have worked with found this an indispensable resource to support inquiry. At the same time, several teachers have asked me how to develop a series of questions for the *ask* stage. In other words, rather than typing a question into a search engine, teachers want to know how to help learners first determine what questions they need to ask and then determine where to ask these questions, be it with a search engine, a person, or some other source.

The second downloadable, *Use These 5 Steps to Learn How to Ask Good Questions* (Crockett, 2017b), breaks the development of questions into the following five steps.

1. **Focus:** What specifically do I want to know? What kinds of information am I missing? Is this more than a simple *yes*-or-*no* question? Am I going for much deeper knowledge? What sources do I have to help me form my initial questions?

2. **Purpose:** Why am I asking this? Do I want to gather facts or opinions? Do I need simple clarification? Do I want to offer a different perspective? Am I looking for general or more specific information? What am I going to do with this information?

3. **Intent:** How do I want people to respond? Do I want the answer to be helpful to others? Am I starting an argument or opening up a discussion? Is the question superficial and not really important or helpful? Am I asking out of frustration or curiosity? Do I really care about the answer? Can I show respect or deference to whom I'm asking?

4. **Frame:** Am I using easily understandable terms or wording? Does my question contain bias or opinion? Is it too long or too short? Does it focus on what I want to know? Is it muddled with other inquiries that don't belong? Does it focus on only one thing?

5. **Follow-up:** Do I have any more specific questions to add? Will the person I'm asking be available for other questions if need be? If I still don't have the answer I need, what are my next steps? What can I do if I still don't understand?

The art of asking meaningful and purposeful questions isn't lost. If we let our students know that, we've given them a great gift. They then have permission to be curious and creative, and they get to think and question in a way that helps them become better thinkers.

Microshifts of Practice: Improved Research Requires Information Fluency

There are a variety of ways you can develop students' information fluency skills to help them conduct their research. In this section, I describe three methods: (1) experiment with advanced search, (2) spot unreliable and manipulative content, and (3) analyze a website's credibility. Each section includes a specific activity you can use with students and reflective questions you can ask yourself about how your students responded.

Experiment With Advanced Search

The advanced search options Google offers allow you to quickly refine your searches by selecting specific date ranges, file formats, language and country preferences, usage rights, and more. Using these features allows learners to produce more focused and meaningful results, avoiding much of the less relevant data that surround the object of their interest.

If you or your students prefer to use search engines other than Google, there are a variety you can choose from that offer similar advanced search features. These include Yahoo (www.yahoo.com), Ask (https://ask.com), Bing (https://bing.com), Baidu (www .baidu.com), AOL (https://aol.com), My Excite (www.excite.com), and DuckDuckGo (https://duckduckgo.com). For students in elementary school or middle school, you can also make use of child-safe search engines like KidRex (www.kidrex.org) and Safe Search Kids (www.safesearchkids.com).

Using sites like these, students can experiment with advanced search techniques to locate, organize, and validate information.

Activity

For students who are already familiar with using search engines and advanced search features, share a topic or a list of topics they can choose from. Ask them to answer specific questions about the topics using advanced search techniques and record their answers for discussion. In addition to recording the information they discover, have them document their experiences with these techniques and share them as part of the discussion.

For students who are new to search engines or are unfamiliar with advanced search techniques, you need to do a bit more legwork to get them familiar and comfortable with these tools as you simultaneously assign them a topic to search. Advanced search techniques are sort of an ongoing study when it comes to using the internet for research. In this case, the best thing to do with learners who haven't logged much or any experience with higher-level search strategies is to let them wade in slowly and learn the basics. If you're using Google, here are some topics to begin with when exploring advanced searching on the web.

- **Explain domains:** Enter a search term or have students enter one. Most any generic search in Google yields hundreds of millions of results. Examine the results you or your students get and highlight websites that end in different domains, such as .com, .org, .gov, and .edu. Explain what these domains communicate about the type of site they apply to. For example, .edu domains usually apply to some form of educational institution or resource, whereas .gov applies to government websites. Most often, .com domains are associated with commercial sites: blogs, news sites, or businesses selling a product or service.

- **Search best domains:** When students understand domains, they can use that knowledge to better target their searches for more credible sources. They can do this by entering the text *site:[domain type]* after their search terms. For example, if students are searching for a specific topic in history, such as World War I, they would type *World War I site:edu* to narrow their search to educational sources and *World War I site:gov* to narrow their search to governmental sources. Note that typing capital letters isn't necessary when using search engines.

- **Search best websites:** When students already know a great resource for finding information on a topic, they can use the same command to further refine their searches by searching only within that site. For example, if students want to find information about a current event such as a recently signed peace treaty and want to use the *New York Times* website (www.nytimes.com), they can enter *peace treaty site:www.nytimes.com*. If your students don't already know what the best sites are, they can use search engines to figure that out too. For example, if they're researching historical information about World War I, you could have them enter the text *best World War I websites* or *World War I websites for students* in a generic Google search. From there, they can use the *:site* command to search within the sites they found, such as *World War I site:www.pbs.org*.

- **Be more specific:** If students are writing a report about a historical topic such as World War I, encourage them to cross-reference and cite from as many sources as possible in their research. One way to do that is to instruct them to use different sources for the causes of World War I, the effects of World War I, and so on. That's why searching for something more specific such as *causes of World War I* will generate much more favorable search results than simply searching for *World War I*. Frequently, more detailed and better-researched sources are in the form of not a generic webpage, but a published document such as a PDF file. Students can restrict search results to a specific format using the *filetype:* command after an entry. For example, they could search for PDFs about causes of World War I by entering *causes of World War I filetype:pdf*.

- **Find specific facts:** The asterisk (*) is another tool that helps students when using advanced search techniques to look for information on the internet. If they're looking for a fact such as a date, they will quickly learn that Google will fill in the blank with information that replaces the asterisk. For example, typing *Austria-Hungary declared war on Serbia on** will yield them more precise results.

- **Find useful functions:** Google is more than just a search engine for finding information, and it features several interesting and useful hidden functions. For example, students can use Google search to find the answers to mathematics problems. Typing *456+456* yields the proper answer. They can also use Google to find the definition of words by typing *define* and then the word they want to know about. Other unique functions students can take advantage of include translate languages (type: *English to Chinese*), find units of measurement (type: *ft to in*), do quick nutritional comparisons (type: *rice vs. quinoa*), search for a number range (type: *motorcycles between $3,000 and $5,000*), learn word origins (type: *etymology:creative*), convert time zones or currencies (type: *convert 5:30 AM GMT to IST* or *convert 1$ to pound*), and so on.

- **Seek specific results:** Students might want to make sure that their World War I report includes information on a key subject by typing *World War I +Franz Ferdinand* in the search box. Similarly, they can use the minus sign to exclude info from the search result, such as *World War I–Russia*. In addition, they can put quotes around a multiword phrase if they want results that feature all the search terms together in that order, such as *"Archduke Franz Ferdinand was assassinated because."*

- **Seek time-specific information:** This tip is particularly important for scientific topics because information is constantly changing. Students who are writing about gene therapy might want to focus on what researchers have accomplished in the last year. They can do that by entering a search, such as *gene therapy filetype:pdf*, and, on the search results page, selecting the *Tools* button on the toolbar beneath the search field. From there, they can use the drop-down menus that appear to refine their search. For example, searches default to the *Any time* setting, but by clicking the drop-down arrow next to it, students can select more restrictive time periods like *Past 24 hours* or *Past year*.

Most search engines provide features similar to these, but specific terminology can vary with the search engine. Beyond search engines, try having learners access information without using a search engine at all. For example, students can search for and locate valid content by using services like Twitter (https://twitter.com) or LinkedIn (https://linkedin.com), both of which they can use to identify and follow subject matter experts who they also have the option of contacting.

Reflection

After you complete this activity with your students, take some time to reflect on and answer the following questions.

- What were their experiences using the advanced search techniques?
- How much quicker were they able to find what they were looking for?
- What did they learn about how search engines organize and rank information?
- Through their searches, what did they discover about online information that they didn't know or expect?

Spot Unreliable and Manipulative Content

A study from the Stanford History Education Group reveals that over 80 percent of students couldn't tell reliable and valid (real) news from invalid and unreliable (fake) news on the internet (Wineburg, McGrew, Breakstone, & Ortega, 2016). It's worth noting that both under-resourced, poorer schools and wealthier ones with extensive research resources yielded the same results. Using information fluency in research means applying critical, analytical thinking to information, especially news consumption. It means developing in students a mindset that encourages them not to take what they see online at face value.

Activity

Collect some stories from both reliable news sites and unreliable news sites. You can find a list of fake sites at https://en.wikipedia.org/wiki/List_of_fake_news_websites; however, do review the site descriptions before activating any links to them. Some of these sites are deliberately designed to infect computers with malware. Once you select some safe (malware-free) sources, present them to your learners and see if they can tell the difference between what is real news and what is fake news.

Because unreliable sources are just as numerous as reliable sources, it's important to help students understand how to avoid being taken in. Here are five practices to share with your learners to help keep this from happening.

1. **Check your sources:** There are many sources and authors out there who are not the definitive experts they claim to be. There are real advantages to the internet being a free and open entity, but that same lack of policing means it's easy to pad an online biography with fictional accolades. A good example is a story that Factcheck.org debunked regarding former U.S. president Barack Obama banning the Pledge of Allegiance in schools (Wallace, 2016). In Wallace's (2016) article, she notes a particular bit of completely fictitious background information that is easy to debunk.

   Students must be certain to acquaint themselves with how to check an author's credibility. If an author does not provide contact information, it may be that the site creators don't want people chasing after them with questions about their content. That alone is cause for suspicion, so have students read the *About Us* sections of sites they research to discern valuable information. It's often easy to tell simply by paying attention to the language writers use. Explain to students that if a site's language is vague or hyperbolic, it could be an indication of an unreliable source. Also have them look for mentions of leadership roles, sponsorship, and mission statements or statements of ethics. These all provide insights into a site's true nature.

2. **Pay attention to URLs:** An established news source will often have its own domain, but copycats are common. For example, when students are rushed, they may not notice a fake URL like *nbc.com.co* or *newyorktime.com* and simply click on it. In these examples, it's the extraneous *.co* or the lack of *s* in *time* that highlights what you want students to watch for. Any simple misspelling of an otherwise well-known name or term in a URL should raise a red flag.

3. **Be wary of ad overload:** An unusual quantity of ads (for example, more than three or four) appearing on a news site can also be a red flag, particularly if the ads have little connection to the products or services offered on that site, or are of a provocative nature with titles such as "You'll never believe what she looks like now!" Such ads are meant to distract,

and they work superbly in that regard. Sites place ads strategically to act as *clickbait*—content designed to attract attention and encourage searchers to click on a link to a particular webpage. These ads generally don't give students a chance to stop and think critically about what they're reading. Although plenty of legitimate sites (especially those of news organizations) do make use of ads, even very intrusive ads, ad overload distinguishes itself by providing the effect of being in a visual candy store with the goal of distracting from content rather than complementing it. Have students stick to sites that focus on the story and not the ads.

4. **Perform a topic search:** If learners aren't sure about a headline or a fact, sometimes the simple solution is the best. Often, they can just search for the topic to see what others are saying about it. A site that posts factual news stories is rarely the only site posting that story, and that often becomes apparent when searching on the article's topic. Have students check to see if reputable news sources are carrying the same story.

5. **Look for the extreme:** Unreliable news stories often make outlandish claims, like predictions of global disasters or stories of miracle cures being "accidentally" discovered. It's good practice to treat any such story with healthy skepticism. Often, there may be some truth in stories that make bold claims. The trouble with them, though, is that these seeds of truth come from a single study or piece of conjecture that the source decided to just run with. The result is a tale that becomes just too good (or too horrible) to be true. Look at some of the other story headlines provided by this source. For example, *Presidential Candidate Suffers Heart Attack* seems like a possibility considering the stress of a nationwide political race. However, if the site reporting it has accompanying headlines like *Man Communicates Telepathically With Dog* or *70-Year-Old Grandmother Gives Birth to Baby Croc*, it's pretty easy to see it for what it is.

It's a fact of life that there is simply a lot of unreliable and untrustworthy information that is readily available for pretty much everyone to consume without question. At best, this can be a minor annoyance, but at its most extreme, it can distort our perception of what is true and what isn't. Once we realize this potentiality, we understand the need for developing the know-how to safely and effectively analyze and apply information for our needs. Ultimately, it is our responsibility to stay informed and enlightened about the truth of what is happening daily in our local and global communities, should we so choose.

Reflection

After you complete this activity with your students, take some time to reflect on and answer the following questions.

- How did your students do on average with discerning unreliable (fake) news from reliable (real) news?

- How could they tell? What were their reasons for the choices they made?

- What made it most difficult for them to realize the differences?

Analyze a Website's Credibility

The internet is an ever-evolving network. Old sites disappear. New ones take their place. When a new site appears, its lack of track record can make it especially challenging to determine its usefulness. It's not always a matter of a site purveying unreliable (fake) content; rather, sometimes a site just isn't very good at producing useful and credible content, even if it's not deliberately manipulative. So, it pays for students to have the skills necessary to determine if a site is worth consulting for practical and credible information. Knowing how to observe a site and make this kind of determination can help students save valuable research time over content that will interfere with their knowledge acquisition and conclusions.

Activity

Whether it's for citations or research, students need a strong grasp of information fluency to determine an internet site's credibility. Mitchell Kapor (n.d.) says it best: "Getting information off the Internet is like taking a drink from a fire hydrant." As teachers of critical-thinking skills, it's up to us to provide guidelines for students to follow when searching for information that's useful. This doesn't have to be complicated, although the more queries a student can make about the viability and credibility of information, the better his or her chances of finding the good stuff. Have students use a quick-reference chart like the rubric in figure 5.1 to help them think critically about the content in front of them.

	Not Credible	Maybe Credible	Strongly Credible
Author	Authors' names are incomplete or nonexistent, making it impossible to search and verify their experience and credentials	For multiple authors, it's difficult to verify their journalistic experience and credentials	Authors' full names are searchable and have verifiable credentials
Current Date	No publishing date	Publishing date provided but not current	Publishing date current and visible
Citations and Links	Links lead to questionable sources; purpose is to gain web traffic to increase ad revenues; quality, current, reliable information is not the priority	Links lead to information to back up the article, but not necessarily a primary or trustworthy source	Citations and links lead to primary or trustworthy sources

Publisher	Publisher found to have questionable credibility and does not take responsibility for the content	Publisher found to be credible, but not necessarily responsible for the content	Publisher visible and searchable; found to be credible and responsible for the content
Other Considerations			
Main Criteria	What is the purpose of the article or website? To sway the reader to a position? To sell a product?		
Accuracy	Are the sources of the article or website traceable to primary or trusted resources?		
Complete- ness	Is the source comprehensive?		
Design and Quality	Is the website easy to use? Is the presentation aesthetically pleasing? Do the design elements serve the purpose of the site?		
	Is this article or elements of it reproduced from another source? Where? Did that source grant permission when needed? Does the article or website cite proper copyright or disclaimer information?		

Figure 5.1: Gauging website credibility rubric.

Visit **go.SolutionTree.com/instruction** for a free reproducible version of this figure.

Whenever your students come across a resource they are interested in using, have them consider the four criteria on the chart. They can then ask the questions under *Other Considerations* to help them quickly analyze the source. Not every criterion will apply, of course, but it's helpful for students to have choices.

Reflection

After you complete this activity with your students, take some time to reflect on and answer the following questions.

- How did these tools work with your students?
- What did students discover about the websites they analyzed?
- What patterns did they see in the design of the majority of websites?
- How can these practices help them in the future?

Summary

As they cultivate their capacity with information fluency, your learners will gain an invaluable set of skills that will help them be not only confident, discerning consumers of information, but also capable, independent, lifelong learners. Now that you can help your learners obtain quality research results using information fluency practices, it's time to see what other essential fluencies they can benefit from using. Specifically, for our next shift of practice, I introduce you to the kinds of process-oriented skills that lie at the heart of solution fluency and explain how you can use solution fluency in your classroom.

Guiding Questions

As you reflect on this chapter, consider the following five guiding questions.

1. What is the definition of information fluency and what are the specific skills it develops?

2. Why are the skills at the heart of information fluency important skills for learners to have to conduct research both in and outside school?

3. What other uses do good research skills have for life beyond school?

4. How do you think the continuing expansion of information creation we are experiencing could shape the future of education?

5. How might students use information fluency skills to determine if a website is invalid (fake) or purveys content that lacks credibility?

chapter 6

Process-Oriented Learning

I have found that all learning requires the learner to apply a process. To conduct a science experiment, one applies the scientific method. Project-based learning, STEM, and inquiry all require processes. In chapter 5, I demonstrate how students can apply information fluency to the research process, but learning has all sorts of processes for tackling all sorts of challenges. It can be about using information fluency to gain a deeper perspective on a profound essential question, solution fluency to solve a complex problem, media fluency to understand the message in media content, collaboration fluency to work as a team, or creativity fluency to add meaning through design, art, and storytelling. That's what this chapter is all about: how *learners* learn to identify a process and apply it to myriad learning applications.

I cannot stress enough that this must be about learners. In my experience, process-oriented learning falls apart in pedagogies such as STEM and project-based learning when the teacher owns the process and guides learners through each step. So, the teacher is doing all the thinking and all the work, and we end up with teacher-directed learning augmented with a form of "edutainment" as opposed to engagement. Conversely, when students know they have a process they can use to solve a problem or achieve a goal, they have everything they require to take responsibility for their own learning. The teacher's role is not more work, but dramatically less because he or she facilitates students' learning by guiding and questioning.

In this chapter, I examine the breadth and importance of process-oriented learning and how students can deploy essential fluencies to achieve their learning goals. From there, I provide three microshifts of practice you can use in your own classroom to help students learn how to identify a process and use it to achieve a learning goal.

The Connection Between Essential Fluencies and Process-Oriented Learning

Consider the following question: What do you do when you don't know what to do? For example, when you have a problem like untied shoelaces, what do you do? Obviously, you tie them—it's a simple problem, and it only requires a simple solution. How about if you didn't know how to tie your shoes—what would you do then? Most likely you would ask someone how. Again, it's a simple problem and there's a simple solution. This simple problem–simple solution mindset is reductionist thinking, and it's a trap people often fall into when deciding on a process to approach a problem.

The reductionist approach is to deconstruct concepts and consider them in isolation. When we don't know what to do, this is often our approach—break the problem down into its component parts until we find a solution. However, it's important to recognize the system, the manifestation of interactions among the various components, may be the issue. Add nonlogical elements such as humans, and the variables increase exponentially as emotion, fear, confidence, stress, or even panic affects a crisis. Russell L. Ackoff and Fred E. Emery (1972) state in their book *On Purposeful Systems*, "Individual systems are purposive, knowledge and understanding of their aims can only be gained by taking into account the mechanisms of social, cultural, and psychological systems."

There is real danger in a purely reductionist mindset. Often, we apply this thinking to all problems, and in doing so not only do we limit our potential, but the outcome can be a cyclical disaster. Consider the following example.

> ***Simple Problem:*** *We don't have enough ethernet outlets in the junior school classrooms for all the devices.*
>
> ***Simple Solution:*** *Replace all the aging computers with iPads.*
>
> ***New Problem:*** *We bought iPads, but we can't use them because our wireless access points can't handle all these new devices.*
>
> ***Simple Solution:*** *Add some more wireless access points.*
>
> ***New Problem:*** *We ordered new WAPs, but when we were installing them, we found that the routers can't be expanded for more WAPs, so we still aren't using the iPads that we bought.*
>
> ***Simple Solution:*** *Install bigger routers.*
>
> ***New Problem:*** *We ordered new routers and have the WAPs connected now, but the new load is too much for the main switch, and we are dropping connections in the senior school as well as the junior school, and now nobody can connect reliably.*
>
> ***Simple Solution:*** *Upgrade the switch to help balance the load.*

> **New Problem:** *We bought a new high-capacity switching system, but the connection to the school isn't big enough for the demand, so we really need to upgrade our service.*

You get the idea. Unfortunately, this is an actual example from a school I was brought in to work with. Worse, it's not an isolated story—I've heard similar stories many times. Often, administrators tell me they are buying iPads for all their students, or they are going 1:1, or implementing BYOD. There's a certain amount of pride that enters the conversation. My response is usually to ask what learning outcomes the school isn't addressing that required the capital purchase, and what the plan is to ensure that the new technology achieves them. It's not a popular question.

The point of this is that an expert problem solver requires both reductionist and holistic approaches. Where reductionist thinking is a mechanical process that does not consider the interrelationship of the component parts, holistic thinking involves considering the big picture and seeing large-scale patterns.

In his book *The Overflowing Brain*, Torkel Klingberg (2009) demonstrates that if a student learns a structured problem-solving process and develops the capacity to use it fluently, he or she gains a 10 percent increase in IQ and sustains this throughout his or her life. Solution fluency is such a process, and if we intend to help students become college and career ready, it makes sense to cultivate these processes to a level of excellence in our schools. The real power of solution fluency is that it and all the essential fluencies we present in *Mindful Assessment* (Crockett & Churches, 2017) are processes that come from the world outside of school—they spring from our experiences in industry applications where we have effectively utilized them.

In the rest of this section, I briefly outline each of the essential fluencies—except for information fluency, which you read about in chapter 5—and highlight how you can help students identify a fluency process to improve their learning and achieve their goals.

Solution Fluency

Beyond college and career, critical thinking and problem solving are life skills. Solution fluency is what you do when you don't know what to do, empowering you and preventing you from being paralyzed by the problem, by fear, by doubt, and by uncertainty. Take a deep breath and always go back to the process; start by defining the problem. My wish is that through solution fluency, every young person builds the confidence and capacity to face any problem with courage, integrity, and compassion.

The following is a brief introduction to the *six Ds* of the solution fluency process. You can find further explanation as well as the rubrics for its assessment in *Mindful Assessment* (Crockett & Churches, 2017).

1. **Define (What do I need to do?):** To solve a problem, learners must first clearly define what the problem is. They need context and a list of potential solutions. Although this includes being able to restate the problem with accuracy and clarity, fluency requires much more. They must also be able to reflect critically and independently on purpose and sequence. This requires breaking tasks down to component elements, sequencing them logically, understanding how to apply tasks and skills to the process, and evaluating completeness.

2. **Discover (What do I need to know and be able to do?):** Learners must decide exactly what they need to solve and give proper context to the problem. Discover is connected intrinsically to information fluency as I detail in chapter 5 (page 59) because it addresses the surface levels of what information fluency explores extensively. It requires developing a series of probing and inquiring questions, as well as accessing a range of suitable and authoritative primary and secondary information sources. Further, students must evaluate the validity of each information source, identify those with the most critical information, and then support them with corroboration from multiple sources.

3. **Dream (What do I want it to look like?):** In the dream stage, learners open their hearts and minds to possibilities and visions of a solution. This phase is about embracing possibilities through imagination, extrapolation, and visualization. Too often, students will limit themselves through negative self-talk. This can arise in the form of self-doubt or more commonly in resisting change by focusing on reasons why not rather than possibilities. In my experience, elementary school students are much less resistant to this process than adults. These students quickly come up with dozens of unique and imaginative solutions, though not all of them are practical or achievable. This is why it is so critical to develop problem-solving skills at an early age. It empowers students to demonstrate what they can do!

4. **Design (How am I going to get there?):** In the design phase, students begin using gathered knowledge to synthesize solutions by starting with a future point in mind and working backward. They create goals and milestones, assign team roles, and create systems of accountability for the whole team. Often people confuse the design phase with the design of a finished product, which is really something that occurs in the dream stage. Design is about creating the process that learners will implement to arrive at the envisioned solution.

5. **Deliver (How do I make it happen?):** Designing a presentation isn't enough; one has to present it. Writing a song isn't enough; one has to record it. Developing a script isn't enough; one has to perform it. Without fully implementing a solution, learners have not solved the original problem and

they do not know if their solution will work. That's where deliver comes in as two separate stages: produce (complete the solution) and publish (present or demonstrate).

6. **Debrief (What were my results, and what did I learn from them?):** During debrief, students look at their projects from beginning to end and really get to own their learning. They determine what they could have done better and ways they could improve their problem-solving approach in similar situations. In taking ownership of the problem, it becomes personal. Because of this, learners have a strong sense of accountability. In my experience, once students have been involved in the debrief phase, they start to "predebrief" by themselves and improve their products before they present them, which is a sight to see.

When students solve relevant problems and critically reflect on their solutions, their process, and their experiences, they engage in deeper learning (Barrows & Tamblyn, 1980). I think of future-focused learning as learners striving together to solve problems that matter as responsible, ethical, global digital citizens.

In the years since Andrew Churches and I first presented solution fluency, I have seen educators implement it far beyond what we intended and to astounding effect.

Media Fluency

Media fluency is about understanding messages in media as well as how people choose to best share those media. It's about knowing your audience, your tools, and your talents. Employing media fluency effectively also requires having a message to share and, hopefully, a purpose for sharing it.

As technology continues to reshape how students think and react to the digital media they consume, teaching media fluency becomes ever more critical to the education environment. This is not an influence you can afford to ignore in your teaching practices. All students should be able to access, analyze, evaluate, and create media in a number of forms through the lens of what I refer to as the *two Ls*. You can find further explanation as well as the rubrics for media fluency assessment in *Mindful Assessment* (Crockett & Churches, 2017).

1. **Listen (What are the message and medium?):** Truly listening to a message delivered via any form of media involves measuring its effectiveness via that medium and decoding its purpose. Understanding the message lets students verbalize in their own words what it is saying while also using information fluency to verify its reliability. Analyzing the medium involves evaluating its form (its design), flow (the logical progression of its content), and alignment (how its form aligns with its message).

2. **Leverage (How do I create a message and use a medium?):** As students learn to constructively listen to media and deconstruct their messages, they can learn to create their own messages by effectively using the media they choose. When crafting their message, they should be aware of their intended audience, know what outcome they're trying to achieve, and know what kind of content they require. Once they select the best medium to contain their message, they should consider the best way to deliver that message in their chosen format, and after they create it, they should reflect on and evaluate their final product's effectiveness.

Strong media fluency skills allow learners to increase their understanding of how media affect society, an essential component of process-oriented learning in a world where much of what students research involves locating and evaluating media sources.

Collaboration Fluency

Collaboration lies at the core of modern learning. Students are familiar with using digital tools for all sorts of collaboration, whether that involves teaming up for school projects or working together to meet a challenge in a video game. Thus, I offer collaboration fluency as the process of cooperatively working in teams with real and virtual partners to create original products.

The following is a brief introduction to the *five Es* of the collaboration fluency process. You can find further explanation as well as the rubrics for its assessment in *Mindful Assessment* (Crockett & Churches, 2017).

1. **Establish (What is this team's dream and challenge?):** Every team project requires a solid foundation, which means establishing who the group members are and each member's areas of expertise, defining each member's role and responsibilities, establishing the information needs of the group, and agreeing on who should lead the group. From here, the group can establish its communication practices, frame its challenge, and outline any project and performance expectations.

2. **Envision (What is our challenge or goal, and how do we meet it?):** In this phase, the group works together to define the problem or situation, visualize the future it desires, specify information needs and identify information sources, and develop its criteria for evaluating the outcome.

3. **Engineer (What is our plan?):** With a vision in place, groups can turn their focus toward engineering a workable plan that establishes how to get from where they are to where they want to be. This involves creating an actual plan that can guide the work, set milestones, ensure communication, and prepare for the unforeseen; and, it involves efficiently delegating responsibilities by assigning tasks based on each member's strengths, dividing

the workload fairly, and allowing team members to rely on each other while developing their individual skills to contribute in a meaningful way.

4. **Execute (How do we put the plan into action?):** With a plan in place, team members can get to work on their assigned tasks. In addition to completing tasks, this phase involves identifying the best format for presenting work or solutions and then doing so.

5. **Examine (What did we learn?):** With the work complete and presented, group members should take time to reflect on how they met (or didn't meet) their challenge and achieved their goals. This includes identifying areas for improvement, recognizing contributions, and giving constructive feedback among members. Students should reconsider each stage of their collaborative process and their final products, reflect on them, and act on those reflections in a way that internalizes what they learned and informs their future work.

For a world in which communication technology plays a starring role, collaboration fluency skills are a huge asset for life after school. One's ability to function in teams that are both real and virtual is important.

Creativity Fluency

Although past experiences may have made them feel otherwise, all students have a wellspring of creativity lying within them that they can tap to produce amazing work, regardless of whether that work comes in the form of design, art, or storytelling.

The following is a brief introduction to creativity fluency as a process utilizing what I call the *five Is*. You can find further explanation as well as the rubrics for its assessment in *Mindful Assessment* (Crockett & Churches, 2017).

1. **Identify (What do I want to create?):** In this step, students should identify the elements and criteria of what they want to create. This involves establishing the problem, identifying key words, forming key questions, understanding any ethical issues, listening to multiple viewpoints and thinking critically about them, and sharing their own knowledge and experience.

2. **Inspire (What inspires me?):** This phase involves students finding or reflecting on any action, encounter, or lively conversation that fires their imagination. It involves moving beyond what they know, using familiar and unfamiliar sources, seeing new possibilities, playing with ideas, and experimenting and imagining.

3. **Interpolate (What are the patterns in what I perceive?):** The brain is a sponge, constantly taking in sensory input and trying to find patterns and connect dots from high-level abstraction. For students, it involves recognizing

patterns, identifying connections and relationships, combining opposing concepts and elements, and thinking laterally about existing knowledge.

4. **Imagine (How do I synthesize inspiration and interpolation?):** This is the phase in which learners cast off extraneous information and zero in on a solution. It is where inspiration and interpolation come together to form an exemplary idea. It involves forming mental images, sensations, and concepts; giving meaning to experience; and being constructive with creative media.

5. **Inspect (Can I make this idea a reality?):** In this phase, students reflect on their idea's effectiveness and feasibility and whether it is something they can accomplish. Sometimes they may find that their idea isn't workable and needs refinement or is something they can put in their pocket to reinvestigate in the future. This phase involves examining the product and the process, comparing and contrasting with the original purpose, internalizing and applying the new idea, and re-examining and revising the idea.

Creativity fluency is a process designed to uncover that artistic nature in all of us, which is critical given we are living in an age in which artistic appeal is becoming increasingly more fundamental to any product's success; one need only look at a company like Apple to see evidence of this. This puts creative people in a position to be prosperous and successful in global marketplaces.

Microshifts of Practice: Solution Fluency Supports Process-Oriented Learning

There are a variety of microshifts you can use that challenge learners to select an essential fluency process that engages them and develops their learning. In this section, I describe three methods: (1) fulfill the dream, (2) master media, and (3) create a group agreement. Each section includes a specific activity (rooted in an essential fluency) you can use with students and reflective questions you can ask yourself about how your students respond.

Fulfill the Dream

Every person has a dream, a goal he or she wants to achieve or an aspiration he or she wants to realize. Often when we can't achieve these things, it's because we feel there is no one to turn to for help, and instead we take an easier or less stressful path that takes us away from our vision. What if you could facilitate your learners in imagining a way to help someone, such as a peer, to achieve a goal he or she has by working together to identify what he or she wants to do and then help him or her establish a process to make it happen? In the case of this particular process-oriented learning goal, the following activity offers an example of having students use the six Ds of solution fluency to give a peer a boost.

Activity

Have students come up with a goal each wants to achieve. Ensure that they use SMART guidelines when stating their goals—they must be strategic and specific, measurable, attainable, results oriented, and time bound (O'Neill & Conzemius, 2006). A few examples of reasonable SMART goals might include wanting to be prepared for an upcoming test, readying an audition piece for a school production, or creating a student-focused monthly media publication. Pair up learners and have them guide each other through an interview process. Because their objective is to learn from each other while helping with achieving each other's stated personal goal, they can use solution fluency to document their journey. Here is how the interviewing student might use the six Ds of solution fluency to formulate his or her questions.

1. **Define:** What is a goal you want to achieve? Why is it important to you? When do you want to achieve it by?

2. **Discover:** What do you know already that would help you move forward? What don't you know that you feel you need to know?

3. **Dream:** What does your perfect vision of you attaining your goal look like to you? How would you benefit from achieving your goal? How would others benefit from you achieving it?

4. **Design:** What is your plan for achieving your goal? How can I help you to achieve it?

5. **Deliver:** What are the first steps you're willing to take toward achieving your goal? How will you know if you are progressing, and how will you manage that progress? What will you do if something isn't working?

6. **Debrief:** What was your outcome, and did you achieve your goal? What could you have done differently?

Obviously, it's up to the person with the specific goal to carry out the actions necessary to achieve it. This activity's purpose is to get learners thinking about how to apply the solution fluency process to something they want to achieve, as well as remove any barriers that may be preventing them from moving forward. In addition, it's a wonderful teamwork and connection exercise that allows students to practice altruism and responsibility for another as they help each other realize a worthy goal.

Reflection

After you complete this activity with your students, take some time to reflect on and answer the following questions.

- How did each pair of learners do with using solution fluency to help each other?

- Do they have a deeper understanding of how the six Ds apply to success in life?

- What were the most challenging areas of this exercise for them?

- What did students learn about what it's like to help others achieve their goals?

Master Media

Learners are passionate about a great many things, and they have a heightened awareness of the world due in large part to the connective technologies they transparently use every day. Smartphones, tablets, and personal computers are part of their repertoire, and each one provides instantaneous access to the sum of human knowledge, as well as a means for them to create and share knowledge and experiences of their own through avenues such as social media. These tools and technologies make it easier than ever for them to share what's important to them with the widest audience possible. The question is, What do they want to say and how?

To that end, ensuring students possess strong media fluency fulfills a number of needs, such as the following.

- They develop critical-thinking capacity.

- They can better identify target markets.

- They can recognize bias and misinformation.

- They hone their ability to distribute personalized media messages.

In the following activity section, I explore just a few effective ideas for lessons you can teach on media fluency.

Activity

You can make a definitive impact on shaping the minds of students and broaden their critical-thinking skills with activities like the following six short activities. In the process, you'll also provide an alternative perspective on media and how students use them. As an added bonus, they can look forward to building other important learning skills such as writing, researching, and analytical thinking.

1. **Picture prose:** Have students view an image of some sort. They should then brainstorm about the events and characters that could be a part of the image. Next, have them write from a character's point of view as they share his or her thoughts, his or her feelings, and the events that led up to the picture or events that will take place after.

2. **Fact or fiction:** Using Snopes (https://snopes.com), have students learn about urban legends and investigate why people believe in them. Use source credibility as a lens to focus a discussion of how students determine whether a source is credible. Students should survey the information they find and identify additional sources to confirm whether a specific urban legend is true or false. Complete this activity with a discussion on how media can shape perception, whether true or false.

3. **What's in a (digital) name?:** For this media-fluency lesson, have students discuss online personas and profiles by researching and discussing their own names and online nicknames. (If they don't have an online presence already, you can suggest existing identities for them to research.) Have them investigate the role their name plays in what they find and what the context of that name reveals about them. Have them use that discussion to determine what name would be most appropriate for social media and email and why it would best represent them online.

4. **Men, women, and media:** Have students explore representations of men and women and discuss their findings. You can have them construct a collage of images that represent men or women and discuss how the media tends to depict each. The idea is to deconstruct those messages by identifying the source and how it may have influenced audience perception. This can get potentially problematic for younger students, because the danger is in them encountering unsuitable content if they're not using a student-friendly search engine (such as Kiddle, KidRex, or Safe Search Kids), or at the very least one with appropriate filters set. Educators should be mindful about how they instruct students to engage in this activity.

5. **Copyright capers:** This lesson explores issues of copyright infringement through the discussion of downloading music from the internet. Have students call upon prior knowledge and experiences on how they retrieve music online and then conduct research to understand the history and legalities of copyright infringement. They should synthesize the information they find and reflect on the legality of their own behaviors and how what they learned affects their point of view. Students should end up taking a stand for their beliefs on what types of downloading or streaming are right or wrong.

6. **Tech reviews:** Have students identify a technology of their choice and employ analytical thinking by researching reviews of that technology. The students should then develop and use a list of evaluation and review questions to think about why people use that technology or why they might use or not use it in favor of a similar technology. Have them write a personal evaluation of the technology and offer recommendations on the audiences it best suits.

We developed these exercises to familiarize students with the aspects of media fluency—in this case, understanding media and how people use media to shape our opinions. There will always be a need for words. That said, images and video alone are powerful enough to communicate our intended messages; our words simply complement them.

Reflection

After you complete this activity with your students, take some time to reflect on and answer the following questions.

- What did you discover about your learners through the messages they chose to share?

- What did they discover about themselves and their own abilities that surprised them?

- How has their understanding and awareness of media changed after this activity?

Create a Group Agreement

The next time your students are working in groups, have them try their hand at creating a group agreement for their project. A group contract is an integral part of establishing a project's parameters and the performance expectations for each member in a group project. It identifies milestones and goals, establishes roles and responsibilities, defines rules and codes of conduct, and ensures that team members have the most positive and productive experience possible while working together. Drafting a contract of this nature involves the learners identifying each member's roles and responsibilities and defining the established norms and the outcome. It can include but is not limited to the group's mission statement, project outline, communication norms, disciplinary guidelines, and more. Not only is this a good opportunity to have students practice collaboration fluency, but its emphasis on accountability and cohesion also makes for good organizational practice.

Activity

Organize students into groups and provide time for them to research group contract elements and experiment with free templates that they can customize to suit their projects and intended outcomes. There are plenty of information resources pertaining to this topic on the website for the University of Waterloo (https://bit.ly/1SksiwY). Then, have each student group pre-examine the following criteria and write up its own official group contract before beginning its next collaborative project.

- **Who makes up the group?** Guide learners toward defining and assembling the core members of their team. Ensure that they include their names and contact information for connecting and working outside the classroom on their own time if they choose.

- **What are the roles and responsibilities?** The group should determine each student's areas of interest and expertise and assign the most effective roles for each team member. In addition, the students will describe the specific responsibilities for each group member, and determine the level of ownership and control group members have. How will the group members make decisions when they can't reach an agreement? How will they go about setting time frames on what gets done when? What will be their procedures for handling disagreements within the group? They should also decide how the group will determine accountability and what will happen if a group member is not demonstrating it as agreed.

- **What are the norms?** Have groups determine how communication will take place and how often members need to communicate with one another. This step is paramount to project success. They may choose to use text, email, or social media exclusively, or they may want to use a team project management application like Slack (www.slack.com), Asana (https://asana.com), or Basecamp (https://basecamp.com). Whatever they decide to use, they must be sure to adhere to structured communication practices and agree to be individually responsible for both communicating to team members and monitoring updates.

- **Who makes up the leadership component?** Who leads this collaborative process and what is the scope of his or her responsibility to the rest of the team?

These are just a few of the things that students could potentially include in a group contract. As they go through this process, think about what skills you want students to learn with this practice. The core focuses for any group contract exercise could include learning personal or group responsibility, accountability, division of labor, project ownership, decision making, goal setting and achievement, conflict management, and more.

Reflection

After you complete this activity with your students, take some time to reflect on and answer the following questions.

- What were the most common components that groups included in their group agreements?

- How did the groups each work together to form the agreement criteria for their teams?

- What were the easiest and most difficult parts of their process?

- What did they learn about group agreements and how they align with collaborative ventures?

Summary

Process-oriented learning with the essential fluencies goes beyond helping students achieve success and be proactive in class and in the working world. Every skill set embedded in the fluencies promotes life success at every level, from the smallest and most mundane of tasks to the most daunting of life's challenges. If we can work to instill these unique skills in our students to the point where they can unconsciously demonstrate their fluency, we prepare them well for the coming challenges beyond school when they no longer have us as teachers. Part of what can help you build these skills in your students is to ensure that, in every lesson, your goals and intentions are clear and that learners have a stake in them by helping you establish them. You'll learn about this shift of practice in the next chapter.

Guiding Questions

As you reflect on this chapter, consider the following five guiding questions.

1. What are the essential fluencies and what role do they play in future-focused teaching and learning?

2. What are the benefits of using the essential fluencies in process-oriented learning?

3. In what ways do you feel you and your learners have already been using essential fluency processes in your lessons? How can you continue to improve and expand on their usage?

4. How do the activities in this chapter highlight using different essential fluencies for process-oriented learning?

5. How else would you like to bring practice with fluencies skills to your students?

chapter 7

Learning Intentions and Success Criteria

In this shift of practice, I will help you understand the importance of making learning intentions clear for students. When you equip students to better understand their goals, they are more likely to do the work necessary to achieve them. I like to illustrate this concept with a short, personal anecdote.

When I was in primary school I wanted to be Spider-Man. I loved the idea of the adrenaline rush and danger of swinging between buildings at high speeds. This is probably what led me to racing Ducati motorcycles in Italy. Really, though, I just wanted to help people; I wanted to make a difference where I saw need. I believe that this desire to do good lies in the heart of us all.

By the time I was in high school, I still wanted to make a difference and I knew it wasn't possible to be Spider-Man; what I really wanted to do was write. I imagined sharing stories and ideas that would inspire people all over the world. I was a fiercely determined student and I announced my intention to be a brilliant writer to my English teacher and attempted to enlist her assistance. She would unlock the mysteries of the written word, and it would become my superpower. Unfortunately, this didn't go as smoothly as it had played out in my mind. We didn't like each other much, and she actively discouraged me, telling me I would never be a writer because I lacked the talent for writing.

As compliance was not in my nature, this, of course, only made me more determined to prove her wrong and perhaps marked the beginning of my journey to want to transform teaching globally. Later, she tasked us with writing an essay comparing *Romeo and Juliet* and *West Side Story*, a riveting topic, and I saw this as my opportunity to show my prowess. I pestered her constantly for criteria about the structure of such an essay—what would make it exceptional, exactly what she was looking for, and by what measure she would mark it. She refused, saying the information was for her to know, and simply told me to submit my work. My essay received a C+ with no explanation as to how I could improve it or what prevented her from marking it higher. I was convinced that it was a masterpiece and that she had treated me unjustly. I brought it to the school principal, who immediately supported the teacher without even reading the essay.

The following year, my friend, who was a year younger, enrolled in the same class and the same assignment appeared. I asked him to write his own, but to also copy mine word for word and submit it first. That same teacher gave the same essay an A+ and held it up in front of the class as an example of outstanding work. She even told the class that he had a promising career as a writer. This is an extreme example, but think about the unclear message this communicates and how it muddies the waters for learning. Was my essay marked down because this teacher didn't like me? Did she mark my friend's version better because she liked him? Things like a lack of clearly stated goals and guidance have a very real effect on students.

My response was to take the two essays, with the grades marked, to the same principal and drop them on his desk as proof of my claim from the year before. The result was a suspension for me and my friend. As far as I know, there were no repercussions for the teacher, although I imagine they discussed it. The effect on me was more dramatic. Shortly after this, though I was a top student, I dropped out of school. I did end up going back, which is a story for another book, but I no longer believed education had much value and thought the system had no integrity. I even went so far as to stage a sit-in at the minister of education's office, demanding he work to change the system—again a story for another book.

Looking back, I confess I feel remorse. Although I had excellent grades, I must have been a nightmare to deal with. I constantly challenged what was fair and just for learners and I'm sure the principal suspended me just to have a break.

Imagine, though, if the teacher had provided me and her other students with clear learning intentions and success criteria, even if she required students to unpack the essential understandings themselves. How might it have influenced my writing, my learning career, and indeed my very outlook on learning? Imagine how it might have influenced other students. Teachers often hold curriculum documents as if they are some mystery that learners are incapable of comprehending. This is just not true and is counterproductive to learning.

In this chapter, I examine the importance of providing learners with clear learning intentions that serve to help them focus their work and engagement to achieve clear learning goals. From there, I provide three microshifts of practice you can use in your classroom to bring more clarity of intention into your instruction.

Examples of Clear Intent

Consider this: I believe one of education's primary goals is to create fully capable, independent learners, and most educators would probably agree. If this is the case, then the easiest teaching job in the school system should be the high school teacher that works with senior-level students. By this point, those learners should be approaching the benchmark of functional, independent learning and only require minor support. However, it seems the opposite is true.

As learners move through the school system, it seems teachers take on more and more responsibility, and we departmentalize and compartmentalize the learning. In most high schools, I find the learners are quite relaxed and the teachers are stressed to the max. Teachers at this level do everything, including unpack the curriculum, develop the lessons, teach the lessons, build the assessments, and so on. They do everything for the learners except fill out the tests, which they might as well do as teachers often must spend so much time test prepping them as well.

Then, once all the intensity is over and our job is done, many of the learners will spend a few months on break before arriving at university, which will expect them to be fully capable, independent learners; they must be in order to be successful in their postsecondary careers. How does this magically happen between the time they graduate and the time they arrive at university? Obviously, it cannot; rather, it must happen gradually throughout their entire learning career. When learners enter the education system at or near age five, they are completely dependent upon us. Our collective goal as teachers must be to ensure that by the time they leave us they no longer need us.

A few years ago, a teacher approached me with a question about the products the students were delivering using solution fluency in his class (T. Smith, personal communication, 2016). He felt everything was going splendidly. The learners were highly engaged and motivated; they were surpassing his expectations by building amazing solutions to relevant real-world problems. However, what they were delivering didn't quite hit the mark for what was in the curriculum, and he was at a loss as to why. When I asked for an example, he said that they were learning about salmon and their breeding habits, but not necessarily grasping the curricular concept relating to the life cycles of living organisms and systems. However, the teacher hadn't exposed them to the idea that this was the intention behind their work. By simply putting the curriculum in front of them at the beginning and unpacking it together, his students would have more consistently achieved the goal he had for them. Even after the fact, however, it's not too late. Think of the concept of herding questions I introduced in chapter 1 (page 9). He could have used their work on salmon to expand on their learning and cultivate a deeper understanding based on that experience.

This example shows what it looks like when a school does not make a concerted effort to ensure instruction provides students with clear intentions. On the other hand, one of the schools I have worked with is St. Joseph's High School in Edmonton, Alberta. Students there self-direct their learning. Essentially, the school presents them with a holistic explanation of the full curriculum goals for all subject areas for the entire year, and students work with a facilitator or learning coach for about twenty minutes a day as they build a plan to achieve those goals.

The facilitator's role is to help them debrief and reflect on where they are in the learning journey and to guide where they go next. The learners have access to teachers in a learning commons—which is essentially a shared learning space similar to a library or large classroom—as one resource, but they largely build their own knowledge and evidence of learning. I should note at this point that this school also offers the International Baccalaureate (n.d.a) Diploma Programme, which is incredibly rigorous. Learners at this school self-direct their learning through this program as well. It's also important to note that these are not learners from a privileged background, and St. Joseph's is not a special school for the elite—anyone in Edmonton is welcome. The atmosphere is calm and relaxed, with learners getting on with the business of learning, in the absence of teachers, with few discipline problems. Interestingly, learners at St. Joseph's on average complete their three years of high school in eighteen to twenty-four months (H. MacDonald, personal communication, 2015).

In 2017, at the renowned Global Education Management System (GEMS) Dubai American Academy, we began the process of working with the high school mathematics department to shift to self-directed learning. Simply put, we placed the learners into groups of three and gave each group a standard directly from the curriculum. Their challenge was to learn it, develop a way to demonstrate their understanding, and teach it to another group. The results were astounding, with learners moving quickly to a very accomplished level. In fact, the class using this strategy quickly became the top-performing mathematics class in the school (Wabisabi Learning, n.d.). This early trial was incredibly successful, and we are working together to determine the next steps for this cutting-edge school.

With all this in mind, consider for a moment students who struggle in traditional curricula and who are not successful by traditional measures—the ones who schools often filter into special classes for learners who are too far behind. In my experience, these are often very talented and capable learners who are completely disengaged from traditional approaches to teaching and learning. I find that these students often don't believe in themselves because they have been unsuccessful and labeled as such, which weighs on them like a permanent judgment of their worth. Given the information I present in this chapter, imagine the benefit for these learners if a teacher or facilitator presented the learning intentions and success criteria in the first few minutes of each class, discussed and unpacked those intentions and goals with them, and then reviewed them at the end of each lesson for feedback and reflection. Based on what I've witnessed at these other schools, I posit that they would learn in that short period of time that they can learn, that they can be successful, and that they can find motivating value in the time they spend in the class. Now imagine further that these students get to repeat this process for six lessons a day, five days a week. How quickly would it transform their view of themselves and their learning?

Microshifts of Practice: Learning Intentions Must Be Clear

Of the ten shifts of practice I present in this book, establishing clear learning intentions may be the easiest to implement. You simply place clear learning intentions about your curriculum in front of your learners and see what happens. I don't think you'll be disappointed. In this section, I describe three methods to accomplish this goal: (1) use know, want, learn charts, (2) begin with the end in mind, and (3) use *May I . . .* questions. Each section includes a specific activity you can use with students and reflective questions you can ask yourself about how your students respond.

Use Know, Want, Learn Charts

Know, want, learn (KWL) charts (Ogle, 1986) are simple and powerful graphic organizers that let students categorize and analyze information before, after, or during a lesson. Use them with your learners to introduce new topics and establish clear learning intentions, reveal prior or assumed knowledge, and share student-designed objectives. These charts are also great critical-thinking tools that get your learners interested in new ideas and subjects.

Activity

Create charts of three columns for each student and give them a chance to respond to the following three questions, either before a lesson or at the end of the lesson as you deem appropriate.

1. What do you know already?

2. What do you want to know?

3. What did you learn?

Figure 7.1 (page 96) establishes a sample chart you can refer to as a starting point for creating your own charts.

As you can see, KWL charts are useful for things like introducing new topics, activating an awareness of previous knowledge, and monitoring students' learning. Using them needn't take much time; it can usually happen briefly at the beginning or the end of a lesson.

Select a topic you want to research. In the first column, write what you already know about the topic. In the second column, write what you want to know about the topic. After you have completed your research, write what you learned in the third column.		
What do I know?	**What do I want to know?**	**What did I learn?**

Figure 7.1: Sample KWL chart.

*Visit **go.SolutionTree.com/instruction** for a free reproducible version of this figure.*

Reflection

After you complete this activity with your students, take some time to reflect on and answer the following questions.

- How was this exercise helpful to you and your students?
- How else can you use these KWL charts in your practice?
- How would you modify them for different purposes?

Begin With the End in Mind

Working backward from the end of the lesson helps you figure out what to make clear about your learning intentions and the students' goals for achieving them by the close of a lesson. Knowing the destination keeps your learners from veering offtrack and gives them a clear picture of the goals they are striving to reach and why they are important. You can do this either by conducting a class discussion or by using individual charts. In either case, the idea is to develop solid criteria for clear intentions and outcomes that everyone agrees on.

Activity

Present students with the prompt, "By the end of the lesson we will . . ." The criteria categories that your learners must respond to include the following.

- Know that . . .
- Be able to . . .
- Understand how and why . . .
- Be aware of . . .

As students respond to these prompts, be aware of how what they respond with defines their own intentions and needs for learning. This is easiest to do with written responses that you can review and act on at a later time.

Reflection

After you complete this activity with your students, take some time to reflect on and answer the following questions.

- How did students' answers to these prompts help you refine your learning goals?
- How has being able to construct and refine learning goals by beginning with the end in mind changed your learners' engagement levels?
- What was the most difficult and the most rewarding thing for them about thinking from the end first?

Use May I . . . Questions

I find it is helpful to keep the discussion open when creating and sharing learning intentions and criteria with your students by providing them with a series of prompts posed as *May I . . .* questions. The process for doing this will vary depending on the age group you work with, but you can apply it to any age group. The learning intentions and criteria should be in constant sight for all learners, and not just something you show them at the beginning of the lesson. This ensures the conversation always remains open about your intention for their learning. From there, establish a set of questions that begin with *May I . . .* or carry that kind of theme (depending on your students' ages) that provides learners with context for asking questions that add clarity to their learning without shifting the burden for learning from them to you.

Activity

At the start of the lesson, provide students with a series of *May I . . .* or similarly themed questions. If you have elementary-age students, use questioning techniques for clarification and understanding, such as the following.

- May I . . . have some more information?
- May I . . . ask you to repeat the question?
- May I . . . have some time to think?
- May I . . . ask a friend for help?

If your students are at higher grade levels, such as in middle or high school, you can lightly modify and adapt these questions to their level, or allow students to use other tactics, like the following, that are more challenging.

- **Present an alternative argument:** Being able to present conflicting viewpoints in a conversational setting can be an excellent proactive communication exercise. Have students ask themselves, "What's another way of looking at the situation that others may not have thought of?"

- **Constructively challenge another's viewpoint:** If there is a conflict of opinion, encourage students to resolve it in a productive manner. Have students answer the question, "What is the flaw in the presenter's viewpoint and how can the presenter address it?"

- **Request expansion of another's viewpoint or opinion:** Often you'll discover students striving to get more clarification on a certain point. If a student feels a certain way about something, ask him or her, "How can you elaborate on your views?"

- **Use full-class debates:** Class debates offer a way to allow multiple viewpoints about an issue or topic to surface and be heard. For truly meaningful debates, you must allow a longer period of time, perhaps a full class period.

We designed these activities to give students a boost to their communication and interaction skills. Additionally, they give students the potential to exercise active listening, which is listening with compassion and true understanding. These skills begin opening doorways to higher learning experiences and can create a sense of belonging for students in our classroom.

Reflection

After you complete this activity with your students, take some time to reflect on and answer the following questions.

- How do these structured questions change how your students think about framing their questions and responses?

- How do these questions help with teaching communication skills and how to relate opinions in positive ways?

- How do these activities guide students in learning healthy and productive ways to disagree with and challenge others?

Summary

It is not unreasonable for students to expect as much of us as we do of them. If we want our students to succeed as much as we say we do (and I believe we all do), then we owe them nothing less than an honest picture of what our goals and criteria are for the learning. But inasmuch as we provide transparency with our learning intentions and clarity of our goals, we must remain invested in a much deeper intention as educators. Our learners must understand first and foremost that we intend to see them succeed and flourish in ways they never dreamed possible and that we stand ready to do whatever it takes to make that happen. This desire for their success lies at the very heart of the next shift, in which I talk about how we can guide our students to go beyond our intentions as they create their own knowledge and learning through curiosity and perseverance.

Guiding Questions

As you reflect on this chapter, consider the following five guiding questions.

1. What questions must you typically answer when creating learning intentions and success criteria?

2. What are the benefits of allowing students to participate in creating their own learning intentions?

3. How can achieving transparency with our learning intentions help those students who struggle more than others?

4. How can using KWL charts and beginning with the end in mind help you provide students with a clearer picture of your goals for them?

5. How can you use *May I . . .* questions to give students paths to engage in their learning in a way that makes their goals clearer and ultimately helps them be more successful?

chapter 8

Learner-Created Knowledge

My work with schools, particularly around the essential fluencies and *Mindful Assessment* (Crockett & Churches, 2017), is focused on moving responsibility for learning to learners. My goal is to build their capacity to be capable, independent, lifelong learners who strive together to solve problems that matter. They must be responsible, ethical, compassionate global digital citizens. They must know how to engage their own creativity to expand their own knowledge and understanding.

Often, teachers and other education stakeholders ask me what the education system is like in Japan. There is a perception inherent in these questions that Japanese education is a factory of long hours of rote learning and heavy discipline. Although I understand how, from the outside, these perceptions occur, in my experience they are far from accurate.

To understand education in any country, you must understand the culture. Part of the beauty of Japanese culture is the sense of responsibility for others cultivated through its customs, religion, and traditions. In schools, it is common not to have janitorial staff; instead the students and teachers work together at the end of the day and leave the school spotless from top to bottom.

People in Japan harbor a deep respect for elders, for ancestors, and for *sensei* (先生), an honorific title used for doctors, spiritual leaders, masters of martial arts, and masters of music and arts, as well as academics and classroom teachers ("Sensei," n.d.). As such, students work very hard for their sensei, who is equally committed to them. On many nights, I have picked up my niece from school late in the evening because in her drive to do her best, she was working with her teachers (who are often still at school to support learners on their own time and by choice) several hours after school ends.

This is a high level of commitment to be sure, but the effort is not related to rote learning and memorization. Teachers in Japan understand that every student is capable of deep thinking and that such thinking is essential to learning. They value wrong answers as much as right answers as these are the gateway to further inquiry and resilience. Education experts often refer to this process as *constructive struggling* (Seeley, 2015). Through constructive struggle, learners extend their own thinking by engaging in tasks and formulating challenging questions.

This learning approach is focused less on the question, How can I teach my students to answer this problem? and more on the mindset shift illustrated by the question, How can I use this problem to guide my learners to understand the mathematics of this unit? To use constructive struggle, teachers intentionally devise methods for slowing down the learning process and postponing a rush to an answer. They instead allow students to grapple with the learning to create their own knowledge. This form of learner-created knowledge is the focus of this chapter. From here, I examine a learning theory called constructivism and how it relates to creativity. Then I offer three microshifts of practice you can use in your own classroom to bring out all students' inner creativity.

Constructivism Leads to Creativity

Constructivism is an expansive and rich learning theory focused on active learning; learners construct knowledge, as opposed to acquiring information (Educational Broadcasting Corporation, 2004). Using a constructive approach, the teacher's role shifts from delivering content to facilitating learning. This shift in practice is critical in a world where we all have access to the sum total of human knowledge in the palms of our hands through digital devices. Limiting teachers to the role of transmitting information is staggeringly inefficient and underutilizes their time.

Constructivism is not a recent practice. It extends back to the Greek philosophers Heraclitus, Protagoras, and Aristotle (The Basics of Philosophy, n.d.). Essentially, we have had constructivist classrooms for as long as we have challenged each other with questions. In modern times, it was Jean Piaget who first offered the term *constructivist epistemology* ("Jean Piaget," n.d.). Piaget along with John Dewey (1933, 1938), Jerome Bruner (1990), and Lev S. Vygotsky (1978) are the major theorists of constructivism.

Studying Buddhism in Japan is like attending a master class in constructivism. Its philosophy posits that there is no absolute knowledge; rather, what exists is our individual interpretation. We therefore construct our own meaning based on our past experiences, our personal beliefs, and our previous knowledge. In this way, we make sense of the world, and therefore, we can never truly understand each other intellectually, as we all are unique. It is at the heart, through compassion, that we are truly able to connect. This is important because it leads us to realize that it is impossible for a teacher to truly be in charge of learning. Our experiences are individual, and we all arrive at the point of new learning within our own constructs of reality and therefore must construct our own learning. Activity and creativity are inherent in this construction.

In this section, I emphasize what brain activity research tells us about the importance of active learning and how that connects to creativity and then use that to follow up with some reflections on why creativity is a serious matter.

Creativity and the Brain

The biomedical engineering division of the Massachusetts Institute of Technology dramatically illustrates the impact of the brain on the construction of knowledge through active learning (Swenson, Picard, & Poh, 2010). The team developed a wearable sensor for unobtrusive, long-term assessment of sympathetic nervous system activity. Participants wore the device for seven days. Figure 8.1 (page 104) illustrates some interesting trends over the weeklong period based on the activity they engaged in.

The high points in a person's sleep pattern are associated with slow-wave sleep, in which the body is healing. However, notice the flat line during class and how similar it is to watching television. Perhaps this is because they are largely the same activity—the passive consumption of another person's thinking. When the students are socializing or even doing chores, there is significantly more activity. Notice the dramatic increases during studying, labs, homework, and an exam, which are most likely due to the increased cognitive load these active learning activities require. These are activities during which learners participate in creating knowledge.

As we wrote in *Mindful Assessment* (Crockett & Churches, 2017), curricula around the world are focusing on skills including creativity, critical and analytical thinking, and problem solving over content. Our learning environments and our governing education bodies must shift to value these transfer skills. This is not a new statement, and seemingly almost every author and every conference keynote connected to education echoes it.

These are not skills students can learn through direct instruction, nor can we test prep for them. They are thinking processes at the top of Bloom's revised taxonomy (Anderson & Krathwohl, 2001) and are exclusive to the individual doing the thinking.

Reflections on the Seriousness of Creativity

Repeatedly throughout this book, I write about the industry demand for creativity. It sounds so serious. In fact, creativity and innovation *are* serious in outcome, but as processes they offer structured play, excitement, curiosity, and wonder.

In Japan, my sensei asked me how I would describe determination (R. Endo, personal communication, 2016). I thought for a moment and said it was a commitment to do whatever it takes to make something happen—that it was about grit, commitment, and the strength to bring something into existence through one's own will even against seemly insurmountable odds. He asked me if I was determined in the work I

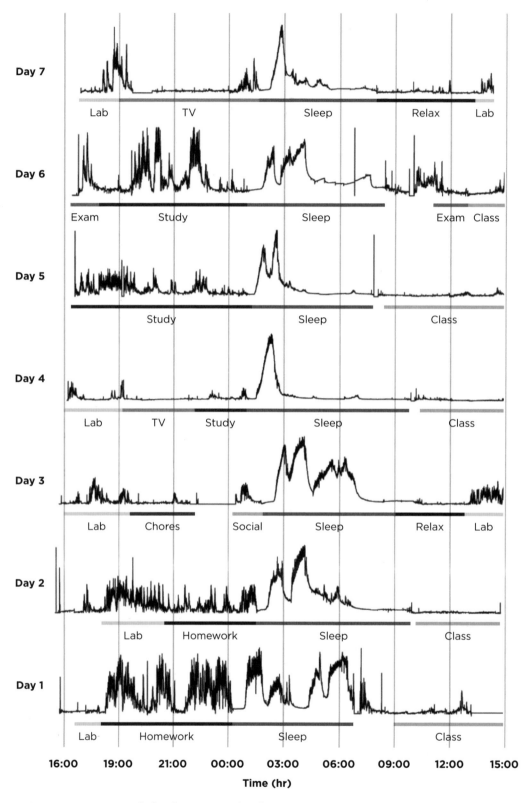

Source: Swenson, Picard, & Poh, 2010. Used with permission.

Figure 8.1: Graph showing an example of sympathetic nervous system activity.

do with schools and teachers, and I said that I was, without question. Then he asked if it becomes tiring doing this work, traveling so extensively, and working so hard to help people and systems transform. I had to admit that it was exhausting, but that I was determined nonetheless. He laughed a little, kindly, and said he felt determination was something different. He believed determination was excitement. That you are only determined when you can see the future so clearly that it is like you are living in that moment—not as a picture, but as a reality in the present. The sights, smells, sounds, and interactions play out for you in your mind in real time. Then, he said, you are so excited about this reality that you can't wait to see what happens in the next moment as you know it is moving you to this reality no matter what. Every moment is something to anxiously anticipate, and challenges are something to greet as welcome friends because they are a necessary part of the journey to the determined future.

In reflection, some of the best moments in my creative career have been when I had this excitement. Creativity is excitement. Some of the best thinking comes out when we embrace our naughty side and do something we know we shouldn't just for the fun of it. An example I often share is of Joel Comm, the inventor of the application iFart Mobile ("iFart Mobile," n.d.). Yes, it is exactly what you think it is, an iPhone application that successfully digitized scatological humor, offering a virtual orchestra of flatulent sound effects. Though the thought of pitching the idea to a group of investors or even close friends seems insane, in 2008 this little application generated sales in excess of $10,000 per day (Hanlon, 2008). Who's laughing now?

Where some see foolishness, others see massive opportunity. There are many examples of high school students, born in the multitouch era, who have sold millions of copies of their applications (Dugdale, 2010). An author can write and publish his or her own book using CreateSpace (www.createspace.com) and iBooks Author (https://apple.com/ibooks-author) and have it listed instantly for sale on Amazon (https://amazon.com), Kindle (https://amzn.to/290v5A2), and iBooks (www.apple .com/ibooks). A coder using Swift (https://developer.apple.com/swift) can develop an application and access a distribution network of millions of customers through the Apple App Store (https://apple.com/ios/app-store) and Google Play (https://play .google.com/store). An inventor can patch together a prototype and raise hundreds of thousands of dollars on Kickstarter (https://kickstarter.com). All of these occur without cash outlay on the creator's part.

Never has there been a time like the one the digital world fosters, when anyone with a creative idea (including students) can bring his or her vision to reality with determination and not capital. Imagine if we allowed students to communicate their understanding and knowledge acquisition in any way that speaks to them or if we allowed them to use their creativity to solve a real-world problem that matters. If our classrooms hold the architects of the future, let them create it now.

Microshifts of Practice: Learner Creation Establishes Focus

You can use a series of microshifts to bring more creativity and active learning into your classroom. In this section, I describe three methods: (1) use a problem-solving scenario, (2) sell an idea, and (3) create a documentary. Each section includes a specific activity you can use with students and reflective questions you can ask yourself about how your students respond.

Use a Problem-Solving Scenario

I have found that one of the best ways to get students thinking is to present them with a problem-solving scenario that genuinely matters to them. You know your students best. Ask yourself what they care about. What is happening in the world or in their community that concerns or engages them? Then, turn them loose with an unlimited mandate to explore solutions to that problem. You will be amazed at what they come up with. For this activity, I selected a scenario that involves school sustainability. You can, of course, use it in full, adapt it, or engage your students in something else entirely.

Activity

Have your students imagine the school board has announced their school is in financial trouble and, to save money, is cutting funding for transportation, school sports, and after-school activities from the budget for the next school year. The school board plans to conduct an open house to discuss possible solutions and you want your learners to get involved in thinking of creating ways to save money without sacrificing learning. Discuss with your learners all the possible circumstances in which the school might be wasting valuable energy sources. This activity will have them complete the following tasks.

- Create a three- to five-minute presentation to the school board profiling the school's energy consumption.

- Identify wasteful resources within the school.

- Suggest a few different ways to cut energy use.

- Suggest alternative resources the school could use and why they are viable alternatives to standard energy sources.

Have students break off into groups and launch an investigation into how the school environment consumes energy. Use previous classroom discussions to inform their research. For example, you may have previously discussed ways people waste energy, so have them figure out which of these things are happening in their school. Chances are, they will discover many ways in which the school is carelessly throwing away energy. They can do this through tasks such as general observations, one-on-one interviews, recording, and note taking.

Your learners can start illustrating the school's energy consumption levels and areas of waste using a number of different illustrations, charts, or graphs for good visual representation. From there, they can move into the ideas they've come up with that the school can incorporate to conserve energy. They should also include a few ideas for possible alternative resources the school could use and explain why these alternatives could save money and be economical enough to implement schoolwide.

As part of this process, have students brainstorm how they want to represent these ideas in a creative and compelling presentation that will get the right people, people with the power to make changes. They will need to illustrate how the conservation ideas will work to cut down on energy costs in the school and back them up with research. Ensure you jot down everyone's ideas and suggestions for consideration in the upcoming design stage. Once this is done, allow them to assign roles to each team member and begin drafting the look and feel of their presentations on energy consumption.

Next, your learners can go through a process of editing, revising, and finalizing their projects. They must ensure that their presentations contain specific examples of how the school is wasting energy and four ways they recommend conserving energy. Remind them that their ideas could become part of a schoolwide energy conservation plan. Once they have revised and polished, they'll be ready to show their presentations in front of the rest of the class. Ask students to think about what their research helped them learn about preserving energy and what the benefits are of doing so.

Reflection

After you complete this activity with your students, take some time to reflect on and answer the following questions.

- How did this scenario inspire students to contribute to cutting down on school waste in cost-effective ways?

- How much total energy do students think the school has wasted over the years?

- Who else can they share their energy-saving ideas with?

- What is the most important thing they were able to take away from this activity?

Sell an Idea

Every idea needs a kick-start, and in a world where great ideas can become reality through digital media, students have the power to develop, publish, and share their ideas with wider and more diverse markets than 20th century teachers could ever have imagined. Let your learners imagine they have a brand-new product that they want to advertise, and they need to figure out the best way to sell the idea. This is something that they will advertise globally in a commercial that will appear on video-sharing sites, television, and social networks.

Activity

For this activity, you want to get learners to design a script and storyboard for a commercial that promotes a new product of their own design. The ideal goal is for them to script and produce a flowing, coherent, thirty- to forty-second digital representation of their own commercial using knowledge they learned in your class. Have them conduct research into effective advertising techniques and study advertisements for ideas on how professionally done advertisements flow. For example, to be effective, the ads must have a central theme that complements the product. They must be creative and eye catching without being overwhelming. They also need a catchphrase to ensure that the ad sticks in the consumer's mind.

Help students get their discussions started by asking them to think about what advertisements they have seen on television or online that are not recent but have stuck in their minds. What is it about them that makes them memorable? Have them think about what commercials and promotional spots led them to purchase an advertised product (or convince their parents to). What was it about the commercial they saw that sold the idea to them?

After this discussion, lead students toward discovering how advertisers use creativity and art in design to bring the company the most sales. Have them inspect many different aspects of creating a commercial. This will include design techniques, use of language, and the unique placement of the product in the ad design and how an ad makes it look irresistible to a consumer. This will help students to promote their own product, which they will work on in the next phase. They can begin to develop these ideas by asking themselves the following questions.

- "What is my product, and what is great and relevant about it?"
- "Why do people need it, and what places it above other products in its class?"
- "How will I grab people's attention and hold it long enough to sell my idea?"
- "How will I use imagery, words, and product placement in my commercial for the most lasting impact on the buyer's conscience?"

Because students will be using every creative talent for design and marketing to create the perfect ad for their product, encourage them to record their ideas as they get them and use them for development notes in the next phase.

To begin bringing their visions to life, have students expand on their product ideas and begin their outlines and storyboards for the commercials they want to create. They will choose to create them in a digital format or use nondigital means and materials. They'll need to produce their first storyboards in this phase as well. They will probably also want the option to use music or a voiceover for their ad design, which is perfectly acceptable. Producing their ads will see them revisit the research they have collected on both effective advertising and the subject they are advertising. When they're ready, they can present their product ideas and the accompanying thirty- to forty-second commercial designs. This presentation should include a clearly stated product idea and it should call on the ad-design techniques that they have researched throughout the phases of the project.

Reflection

After you complete this activity with your students, take some time to reflect on and answer the following questions.

- What did students learn from the other projects that they saw?

- Have they been able to share their ideas effectively and inspire each other with their own creativity?

- How has this new learning made a difference to them in terms of looking at ads more critically?

- Do they feel they have become better at recognizing the messages and marketing strategies companies use?

Create a Documentary

Documentaries are an excellent way to merge creativity and knowledge acquisition. By having students produce a movie, a webpage, a podcast, a poster, a brochure, or another resource to help inform their community about an important topic, they can put their learning to work in productive and creative ways that demonstrate their learning. For example, many of us want to know about the risks of extinction for numerous endangered species across the world. So, you could challenge your students to explore ways to inform their local community of the danger of extinction facing numerous species of animals at the hands of humans by producing informative segments that both educate and inspire.

In addition to the core learning and creativity on display, having students educate people about a topic or problem of interest in their community will help promote local and global awareness of this problem. Are your learners up for the challenge?

Activity

In this activity, have learners work in groups to identify animal species on the brink of extinction; research the animals, their habitats, their food sources, and the specific cause or causes of their endangered status; and offer innovative suggestions for safe-guarding them from extinction. Each group can produce a product of its choosing to inform the community about the animal's plight. (If you prefer to use another topic area of relevance, you can adapt this activity accordingly.)

Help learners begin by identifying a species characterized as endangered and research its attributes to inform the documentary audience. This could include the answers to the following questions.

- What does the animal look like?
- Where in the world does it live?
- What is its habitat?
- What is its behavior like?
- What does it eat and what eats it?
- What are some interesting facts that make this species special?

Next, ask learners to describe the creature's plight. Have them define the dangers to the species and research potential solutions to broadcast to the audience. This phase should involve students asking each other and themselves questions like the following.

- What is endangering the species?
- Are humans to blame?
- How can humans change these harmful factors to help the species thrive?
- What actions must humans stop or start to protect this species?

In addition to this exploration, have your learners closely observe some documentary clips to become familiar with the style of how a documentary presents its content to the audience.

As students begin to sketch out their documentary ideas and prepare to create content, have them consider questions like the following.

- What information about the animals will audience members find interesting?
- How will the information the segment presents help audience members develop a better understanding of the dangers of extinction?
- How should students outline the information in the script?
- Why will an informed audience make the decision to change something to protect these animals?
- What will happen to these endangered species if humans take no action?
- If the animal becomes extinct, will it impact humans or the Earth?

In this stage, students can create the script with the information they discover during their research. Scripts can go through a peer-review process, and you should give them time to rehearse in preparation for recording their segment. Remind students to speak in a clear tone with no hesitation, encourage them to take turns listening to their group members, and coach them with appropriate feedback and suggestions to strengthen their delivery. Students should combine their recorded narration with species images or video clips to produce a finished documentary segment. Students should splice together all segments to generate a finished and cohesive documentary episode they can then share with peers for feedback and critique.

Reflection

After you complete this activity with your students, take some time to reflect on and answer the following questions.

- What are the causes of endangerment and extinction?

- What are some potential courses of action we can implement locally to help endangered species across the world?

- What actions do learners want to take now that they are aware of some of these problems with endangered species?

- What solutions are easy to implement and which ones will be a challenge?

Summary

As you move forward with a classroom focused on tasks that encourage your students' creativity, you will see remarkable changes slowly begin to take place. You'll see their desire to learn increase as interest takes center stage. Their search for answers to problems that stimulate their creative minds will transform them into agents of discovery and lead them to deeper learning and more in-depth inquiries. Most of all, you'll watch as your learners realize that learning is all about exploring their potential and fulfilling possibilities both in and out of the classroom. These changes go hand in hand with how your assessment of learning processes and tasks will also change, which is the shift of practice you will explore in the next chapter.

Guiding Questions

As you reflect on this chapter, consider the following five guiding questions.

1. What does the term *constructivism* mean from an education standpoint, and why is this significant for the transformation of learning?

2. What are the benefits of slowing down learning?

3. Why is it important for students to be able to construct their own insights and knowledge?

4. How can you use a problem-solving scenario to engage students in a topic of concern to them or the community in which they live?

5. What are the benefits to student learning in having them use their creative skills to sell an idea?

chapter
9

Mindful Assessment

Learning is and always will be a journey characterized by as many hills and valleys, as many endless winding curves, and as much struggle and victory as any other journey in our lives. This is indeed what learning is like for the digital-age learner living in a world that's changing as rapidly as ours, and with education systems that are racing to adapt to these changes. It makes us forget that teaching and assessment were once much simpler and more straightforward.

Using traditional forms of assessment, we mark our students in their education journeys using what amounts to a simple number or percentage. Educators intend for these numbers to be helpful and provide a snapshot of where students are in their learning. Providing nothing more than a numerical value, however, is an incomplete measure of cognitive ability, learning capacity, and creativity. It neither identifies strengths and weaknesses nor provides essential, constructive, and actionable feedback for learning and development. It is finite, and it marginalizes the holistic side of our learners that we need to understand so we can adjust instruction to help each student both excel and fulfill outcomes. Nevertheless, throughout the years, our schools have sent countless students out into the world armed with a percentage and a mindset of, This is what I'm capable of, and this is the best I can do. It's astounding to reflect on the amount of untapped potential this represents.

As educators in the modern digital age, learning and how we assess it must transform dramatically. There are myriad ways in which we've strived to do that (Wiliam, 2018). We are accommodating learners who think and perform on a whole new frequency because modern students require a unique kind of assessment process, one that is relevant to instruction in the digital age, and also mindful in that it focuses on adaptation, continual adjustments, and fostering a learner's growth and progress.

What we do know for certain is that it is only the learners, and not the educator, who create learning. An educator cannot learn for a learner any more than someone can lose weight for another. It is the teacher's role to guide the learning process by responding to his or her learners' performance. This happens through designing the very best kinds of modern learning assessments possible and using them to help students improve and excel as they learn. The practice of mindful assessment, the topic of this chapter, helps teachers do this. I explain what makes assessment mindful and provide microshifts of practice you can use in your classroom to improve your assessment practices.

How Assessment Becomes Mindful

It is impossible to summarize the content of the book *Mindful Assessment* (Crockett & Churches, 2017) in a single chapter. This shift of practice contains many elements. However, when I talk about mindful assessment, it's best to get a clear idea of what mindfulness means and especially how it translates to assessing our students. Basically, you could call *mindfulness* being conscious and present, and clearly seeing the situation before you by focusing on the one and only moment that matters, which is *right now*. Why? Because *now* is the seat of our power; *now* is the time to take decisive action; *now* is the time to begin meaningful change. Not tomorrow, not three months or ten years from now, but right *now*.

When it comes to learning, our best assessment opportunities happen in the now, the precise moment in which a learner is struggling and willing to rise higher, and not during the final exam at the end of the year. This means shifting our idea of assessment from being a passive grading exercise to being an immediate response to learning, with mindfulness as the method by which the learner improves. In short, we should not see learning as the outcome of teaching, but rather allow teaching to become a mindful response to learning.

When we are assessing mindfully, there are four key things that should happen.

1. We observe and pinpoint what must improve.

2. We provide constructive feedback.

3. We provide a demonstration of the new learning path.

4. We step back and provide each learner with the opportunity to improve.

The two types of assessment that largely concern us as educators are *formative assessment* and *summative assessment*. Formative assessment occurs throughout a course or project. Also referred to as *educative assessment*, teachers use formative assessment to aid learning. In an education setting, formative assessment might be a teacher, a peer, or the learner providing feedback on the learner's work and is not necessarily something you use for grading. *Summative assessment* is generally something you carry out at the end of a course or project. In an education setting, teachers typically use summative assessments to assign students a course grade. These types of assessments are generally evaluative. In other words, summative assessment is assessment *of* learning, and formative assessment is assessment *for* or *as* learning (Chappuis, Stiggins, Chappuis, & Arter, 2012).

Though acceptable for reporting and compliance, summative assessment is not ideal for learning. For example, Dylan Wiliam (2018) points out that when learners see a number, it signals the end of their learning because they see it as a nonnegotiable, summative judgment of performance. In other words, summative assessments inherently foster in learners a fixed mindset (Dweck, 2006). Formative assessment fits much better with regard to learning because summative tells the learners what they have done, but formative tells the learners what to do to improve (Crockett & Churches, 2017). Formative assessment and feedback, when educators use it appropriately, is the only form of assessment that can improve learner outcomes. It builds in the needs and expectations of students growing up in a digital age, and it works within the teaching and learning outcomes schools have in place.

One of the best things about incorporating mindful assessment into your teaching practices is that it needn't be complicated. You can perform ongoing assessment using simple in-class tools and approaches that allow learners to assume direction and take control of the task, leaving you in the ideal position of being facilitator and guide for positive change in the classroom. No matter what kind of assessment task you design, you can refine it using the following four criteria.

1. **Assessment should be goal oriented:** Goal-oriented assessment derives from what we do every day. Use it to guide students toward performing well. It should be specific, observable, and measurable. For example, statements such as "Learners can count by twos" or "Learners will be able to explain how metaphors create understanding" are goal oriented.

2. **Assessment must focus on higher-order-thinking skills:** Assessment that focuses on higher-order-thinking skills is not about just the facts and figures. You want to know if students are applying, analyzing, evaluating, and creating (Anderson & Krathwohl, 2001).

3. **Assessment should hold students accountable for *individual* performance:** Group assessment is useful in itself and fosters a shared learning culture, but you must also consider an individual's performance within a group. Doing so pinpoints the exact needs of the individual and gives you direction to steer your instruction. This sets the learners up for success.

4. **Assessment should be seamless:** Formative assessment should be part of the ebb and flow of learning, instead of the start-and-stop practice of teach, test, and move on to the next unit. Providing learners with formative feedback and activities to allow them to implement the feedback they receive should be a regular structure of learning. Some formative assessments have a steep learning curve, while others are easy to grasp even with the most limited experience. Depending on the complexity, formative assessment can simply be part of a lesson you conduct, something you improvise, or a process you plan out far in advance.

Microshifts of Practice: Assessment Requires Mindfulness

Making your assessments mindful is something you can do regardless of curriculum or your instructional pedagogy. In this section, I describe three microshifts of practice you can use: (1) conduct peer interviews, (2) submit one-minute papers, and (3) use creative extension projects. Each section includes a specific activity you can use with students and reflective questions you can ask yourself about how your students respond.

Conduct Peer Interviews

Peer interviews are a mindful assessment technique you can use to personalize learning for students as well as allow them to take ownership of it. Like many shifts, it overlaps with other shift concepts and you will find similar activities in chapter 10 (page 121). This specific activity is similar to think-pair-share and happens at the end of the class (Simon, n.d.).

Activity

For this activity, have pairs of students take a few minutes at the end of class to discuss what they've learned. Each student should take a turn interviewing the other. You can give your students guiding interview questions to use with each other such as the following.

- What was the most useful thing you learned?
- What did you struggle most with?
- What will you ask for help with next class?
- What can you do to help somebody else learn better?
- What's your learning goal for next class?

Students can continue working with their interview buddies to help keep each other on task for the upcoming lessons and act as mutually supportive learning partners for as long as necessary.

Reflection

After you complete this activity with your students, take some time to reflect on and answer the following questions.

- What does this collaborative activity show students about helping others?

- How does this activity provide ongoing peer assessment opportunities for students?
- How else could you use interviews and learning partnerships with your students?

Submit One-Minute Papers

Without formative assessments, the first indication that a student doesn't grasp the material is when he or she fails a summative assessment such as a quiz or a test. An innovative formative assessment strategy like one-minute papers can take failure out of the classroom. Using this activity, students can work individually or in groups to answer a set of brief (one-minute) questions in writing.

One-minute papers can help you take a quick snapshot of the effectiveness of the day's learning, and they can reveal to students where their true learning interests lie as well as what they are most curious about. You can use one-minute papers at any point throughout the day, but they work well as exit tickets right before the class leaves for the day. This is a wonderful reflection exercise that can help you take the class in interesting directions once you discover what students are intrigued about learning.

Activity

The key aspect of having your students engage in a one-minute paper as a formative assessment is that you carefully choose the questions you ask. They should be easy for learners to comprehend and allow them to provide fast, simple answers. Typical questions could center on the following aspects of their learning.

- The main point
- The most surprising concept
- Any questions not answered
- The most confusing aspect of the topic
- What question from the topic might appear on the next test

For this activity it's best to attain written responses that you can review later. There is an even simpler version of this activity you can use more frequently if you desire. At the end of a class, take time to give students blank cards or paper and have them write responses to the following two questions.

1. What was the most significant thing you learned today?
2. What question is still uppermost in your mind?

Experiment with other questions that you can ask your students at the close of a lesson. Another variation of this is 3–2–1, where you ask your students to list items such as three things that interested them, two questions they have, and one thing that surprised them.

Reflection

After you complete this activity with your students, take some time to reflect on and answer the following questions.

- What skills do activities like these help your learners develop?
- How can you use the information you gather to revise your lessons?
- What other questions can you devise for this activity that will help you best assess your learners?
- How can you refine this activity to be even more challenging?

Use Creative Extension Projects

Creative extension projects are projects that are intended to demonstrate comprehension through high levels of creativity. Such projects help learners apply the higher-order-thinking levels of Bloom's revised taxonomy, the highest of which is, of course, creation (Anderson & Krathwohl, 2001). These don't have to be big and complicated. You can have students take a day, a half-day, or even just an hour to create them.

Activity

Because these extension projects are meant to be creative and engage students in active learning, there are any number of directions you can use to get your students involved in making them. Here are some extension ideas for projects that allow learners to demonstrate their understanding.

- Create a poster or collage illustrating the subject.
- Record or rehearse a podcast or skit discussing a topic.
- Build a diorama about the subject and create a narrative behind it.
- Design flashcards to test peers with.
- Make keynote presentations on the topic.

When choosing or developing projects for your learners, keep these considerations in mind.

- What do I think my learners value about the extension projects?
- What criteria should I use in my assessments of the projects?
- How can I involve students in establishing the assessment criteria?

- What would a checklist that identifies the evaluation criteria look like?

- How can I guide my learners toward appropriate self-reflection?

Reflection

After you complete this activity with your students, take some time to reflect on and answer the following questions.

- What different skills can you develop with your students by modifying these activities?

- What other activities can you think of for creative extensions?

- What are the benefits of involving students in the assessment building process?

Summary

How we mindfully assess our students is important but even more important is how they assess themselves and each other. The fact is that we are only with our students for a short time; the rest of the time they are revising and improving on their own, becoming the responsible lifelong learners we want them to be. Love of learning is a worthy goal for us to want our students to achieve, but what should accompany that passion for learning is a keen ability to engage in useful assessments of their own so they can continue understanding what they are missing and where they may need to improve. That's why in the next chapter you're going to learn about my final shift of practice, which is self- and peer assessment.

Guiding Questions

As you reflect on this chapter, consider the following five guiding questions.

1. Why do we assess learning?

2. How best can we use assessment to improve learning?

3. What is *mindfulness* and why is it important to our assessment practices?

4. Why is formative assessment the most ideal form of assessment for modern learners?

5. How can you use practices like peer interviews and creative extension projects to gather formative assessment data that improve your instructional practices and student learning?

chapter 10

Self- and Peer Assessment

Whenever teachers or other education stakeholders ask me about assessment, my first response is to ask, "Why are we assessing?" Often, I hear that the goal is to improve learning. As I establish in chapter 9 (page 113), if that's the case, then we should be working strictly in formative assessment. In my experience, it is the only format that consistently improves learning outcomes. The response is usually that the school or district has to report on student learning, but this reveals an uncomfortable truth: such assessment is not about improving learning but about reporting, and without feedback, assessment is not a learning activity; rather, it is a compliance task. It is something we do *to* students, not *with* them.

The next question I ask is, "How are we assessing?" It is here that we often miss a substantial opportunity. Even when assessment is mindful, I see schools too often pass up opportunities to involve students in the development, application, and reporting of assessment. In his book *Visible Learning*, John A. C. Hattie (2009) states that self-reporting grades comes out at the top of all influencers of academic performance. This is why this final shift of practice focuses specifically on formative assessment practices that get learners involved in self- and peer-assessment activities.

The Case for Self- and Peer Assessment

I often encounter substantial resistance when I posit getting learners more involved in their own assessment. Teachers resist this in a variety of ways, and I understand the trepidation in relinquishing control of assessment to learners and the concerns many educators have that their learners may not be capable of such a task. It seems such a crucial part of a teacher's role, especially given that assessment reflects on not only the learner but also the teacher, and districts and states often use it as a measure of teacher performance. There is much I could write about this but let me simply point out one thing: I stated that learners should be involved in development, application, and reporting of assessment. This notion leaves out that the most essential role in this process is the one left for the educator, who is the moderator of the assessment. The moderation role ensures that assessment is accurate and consistent between learners and between classrooms and provides learners direction as to how and why an assessment should be modified. Contrary to what you may expect, in my experience learners are incredibly tough on their own work and that of their peers. What they need is guidance as to how to assess fairly.

Hattie's (2009) work cites five metasources that he used in reaching his conclusion that learner involvement in formative assessment leads to better outcomes: (1) Paul A. Mabe and Stephen G. West (1982), (2) Nancy Falchikov and David Boud (1989), (3) Steven Ross (1998), (4) Nancy Falchikov and Judy Goldfinch (2000), and (5) Nathan R. Kuncel, Marcus Credé, and Lisa L. Thomas (2005).

There are many other sources that also support self-assessment. For example, Dirk Campbell, Lora DeWall, Trenton Roth, and Sharon Stevens (1998) state that self-assessments "provide students with a greater sense of ownership of their work, a more enthusiastic approach to learning, and the increased use of higher-order thinking." Most every school I have worked with has stated these outcomes as criteria they want to achieve. Further, Susan M. Brookhart, Marissa Andolina, Megan Zuza, and Rosalie Furman (2004) note, "Motivation theorists suggest that student self-assessment will contribute to feelings of control over one's own learning, of choice and of agency, and of self-worth." They go on to point toward a recommendation from the Assessment Standards for School Mathematics from the National Council of Teachers of Mathematics noting the importance of "student self-assessment as part of a total assessment plan to foster student confidence and independence in learning math" (Brookhart et al., 2004).

In "The Student's Role in the Assessment Process," Richard Wells (1998) indicates that self-assessment "gives students ownership of their own learning and provides them with a means for evaluating their growth and setting goals for the future" (pp. 32–33).

When we think about these statements, they seem obvious. In chapter 7 (page 91), I wrote about the importance of clear learning intentions. Specifically, I related the saga of my *Romeo and Juliet* and *West Side Story* comparison essay and how the lack of objective clarity negatively affected how my teacher assessed it as well as my understanding of the task and thereby inspired me to leave school. I can only imagine how I would have performed on that task if the assessment had been clear, fair, and transparent, and if the teacher had then asked me to apply my own assessment to my work. I have come to the same conclusions in my own teaching experience as the researchers I cite in this section—learners are much harsher in assessing their own work than we would ever be, and that leads to them working harder to improve.

Self-assessment does not have to be a massive undertaking; it can start as simply as setting up the debrief in a solution fluency challenge by creating evidence statements or in co-constructing success criteria after establishing clear learning intentions. It is clear that this shift of practice has the potential to make the most substantial impact on learning, and learners are never too young to get involved in the process.

Microshifts of Practice: Self- and Peer Assessment Benefit Learning

You can use a series of microshifts to involve students in their own assessment. In this section, I describe three methods: (1) establish a self-reflection journey, (2) answer fifteen questions, and (3) implement trade-off 2–1. Each section includes a specific activity you can use with students and reflective questions you can ask yourself about how your students respond.

Establish a Self-Reflection Journey

Reflective learning is something that takes time; it demands thought and effort. Most often, teachers conduct a debrief or learning reflection after the lesson is over and students have already applied the process. However, there are other opportunities for students to self-reflect and assess themselves throughout the learning progression. Establishing ongoing and effective self-reflection sets learners on a journey that contributes to higher levels of self-awareness, meaning they get better at pinpointing not only where they are succeeding but more importantly where they need to improve as they continue to learn.

Activity

At the beginning of a lesson and then throughout the learning process, encourage learners to mindfully explore reflective questions like the following.

- Am I asking questions while I'm learning?
- Am I formulating answers while I'm learning?
- Am I investigating answers to my questions?
- Do I understand the importance of what I'm learning?
- Am I becoming more curious about what I'm learning?
- Can I add something to my teacher's explanations?
- Can I challenge conventional points of view?
- Can I communicate different points of view?
- Are my communication skills improving?

When learners reflect on a project, they reflect on everything, including the process, the choices and discoveries they made, and what didn't go quite as expected. It's when they piece them all together into a learning experience—even one or more aha moments—that self-reflection becomes useful.

It's worth noting that the six Ds of solution fluency lend themselves well to reflective learning (see page 77, Solution Fluency). Indeed, the define, discover, dream, design, deliver, and debrief process takes students through a full cycle of constant self-reflective learning and improving. By incorporating systems like the six Ds within the learning structure in a way that inspires reflection, we can instill in ourselves and our students good habits of mind and lifelong learning skills.

Reflection

After you complete this activity with your students, take some time to reflect on and answer the following questions.

- How did this self-reflection practice boost learning for your students?

- Where else, other than the classroom, could learners use such questions?

- Given the opportunity, what other self-reflection questions can your students come up with on their own?

Answer Fifteen Questions

Having students successfully debrief their learning means having solid and meaningful reflective questions to use. No matter what you're teaching, all learners can benefit from asking reflective questions at the end of their journey because these reflections help develop their critical-thinking skills, foster lifelong learning mindsets, pinpoint areas for improvement, increase self-awareness, and more. So, it's very important to ask the best reflective questions possible as you debrief students on their products and processes.

Activity

Use the following fifteen questions as an end-of-class, -semester, or -school-year debrief session. Although I wrote these primarily for high school–level students, you can adapt them to suit any age group.

1. Define some of your most challenging moments. What made them so?

2. Define some of your most powerful learning moments. What made them so?

3. What would you say is the most important thing you learned personally? As a team?

4. When did you realize that you had come up with your final best solution?

5. How do you feel your solution relates to real-world situations and problems?

6. What do you feel most got in the way of your progress, if anything?

7. How well did you and your team communicate overall?

8. What were some things your teammates did that helped you to learn or to overcome an obstacle?

9. How did you help others during this process?

10. Did you mostly meet your milestones and goals, and how much did you deviate from them if at all?

11. What did you discover as being your greatest strengths? Your biggest weaknesses?

12. What would you do differently if you were to approach the same problem again?

13. What would you do differently from a personal standpoint the next time you work with the same group or a different one?

14. How can you better support and encourage your teammates on future projects?

15. How will you use what you've learned in the future?

These are questions you must encourage and guide your students to deeply ponder. Thoroughly discuss them with your students and help herd them to self-assessed conclusions that will improve their understanding and work going forward. In a safe learning environment (like yours), the results will astound you and your learners.

Reflection

After you complete this activity with your students, take some time to reflect on and answer the following questions.

- How did these questions connect your students to their learning experiences in ways they hadn't before?

- What did students learn about themselves through these questions?

- What other questions could you add to this list to ask your students?

Implement Trade-Off 2–1

To have any meaning, assessment feedback and conclusions must be proactive and actionable. Too often, I see teachers give students a number or a percentage even on assessments they mean to be formative, which is an inefficient indicator of both their learning capacity and what they need to improve. Implementing a trade-off 2–1 activity gives your learners a chance to review each other's work in a supportive way and put the feedback they receive into practice, giving them new insights into their own work they may not have previously considered. The 2–1 aspect refers to the feedback given during the assessment, which is two pieces of constructive criticism and one suggestion for improvement. When students have a chance to have someone look at their work in this way, they receive an entirely different perspective from their own or yours.

Activity

In this activity, have students break off into pairs. Each student then reviews the work of the other and offers two pieces of constructive feedback and one suggestion for how his or her peer could improve it. Give students enough time to implement the suggestions into their work so they can see firsthand how the feedback they receive impacts that work.

In my experience, the questions learners ask each other on their own and without prompting are ones that encourage their peers to think critically and creatively. Expect to see them ask each other questions such as, "This is really great, but what if you added this?" or "I see what you were going for here, but what if you tried this and compared them?"

Reflection

After you complete this activity with your students, take some time to reflect on and answer the following questions.

- What did this exercise teach learners about the importance of both giving and receiving appropriate feedback?

- What did they discover about their own work from the feedback they received?

- What are some of the areas they are strongest in, and what would they like to improve?

Summary

If we are to develop capable, lifelong, independent learners, it is essential that they have the ability to evaluate and reflect on their performance. Being clear on what a quality outcome would be and how to recognize it obviously has the potential to contribute greatly to accomplishing this. Self- and peer assessment put the learners at the center of the learning and help them be accountable and self-reliant. Although it may be a significant professional challenge to make this shift, it is among the most important and impactful actions you can take to improve your teaching practice as it is one that is most truly focused on each learner's future.

Guiding Questions

As you reflect on this chapter, consider the following five guiding questions.

1. What are the benefits of learners practicing regular self- and peer assessment?

2. In what learning situations could self- and peer assessment be most effective?

3. How does this kind of assessment align with today's innovative learning environments?

4. Why do we need to ensure our learners can assess their own performance?

5. What implications do self- and peer assessment have for learners' lives beyond school?

Epilogue

As I write these words, our home in Japan is very busy. It is New Year's Eve and this time of year is very different here than what I grew up with in Canada. It is a time when this modern, high-tech country turns to custom and tradition. On December 31, families traditionally prepare a dinner of soba (buckwheat noodles). As the old year fades, the temple bells ring 108 times, and crowds gather to offer their prayers for the new year. With each toll of the bell, one of the 108 human desires, believed in Buddhism to be the cause of all suffering, is removed, leaving people cleansed to begin the new year.

The last few weeks here have been bustling with activity, and New Year's celebrations do not end until January 15. During December, there are many parties as people get together to let go of the old year—both the good and the bad. People here expect to let go of unresolved conflicts rather than carry them forward into another year.

In the *Shinto* tradition, Japan's indigenous religion, the *kami* (gods) enter the house at New Year's. Because of this, families conduct a complete cleaning of the house (*Susuharai*) from top to bottom, literally from the attic to the floors under the tatami mats. Schools close on December 25, not for Christmas (it's not celebrated here), but because on this day everyone, even children, is involved in the cleaning and the final, intense preparations for New Year's.

I can smell the *soba* cooking now as we let go of the past and focus on the future. It's fitting that it is today that I am finishing this book, reflecting on the challenge of transformational change and considering why it is so seemingly difficult in education as compared to other organizations. I believe this is largely due to the fact that most educators have spent their lives since the age of three to five inside a classroom. Therefore, many educators have experienced teaching, learning, and assessment models for six to eight hours a day for fifteen to twenty years before ever standing in front of a classroom. Is it any wonder that shifting practice is so challenging? It equates to telling someone the way he or she is walking or breathing needs to change, as there are few other things he or she has spent as much time doing.

With this in mind, we need to be compassionate with ourselves and with each other, with a healthy dose of humor (and a decent serving of *soba*) as we strive together to transform education. If we adopt the mindset of *wabisabi*, that nothing lasts, nothing is finished, and nothing is perfect, we can reflect on our practice with pride yet without attachment and constantly refine toward a vision of future-focused learning. It's time for us to let go of the good and the bad, envision what kind of future we want to create together, and ensure it's realized. Let's together clean our house from top to bottom, celebrate our past, and embrace our future.

Appendix
Additional Microshift Ideas

What follows in this appendix is a list of additional microshifts to supplement the ones we've profiled in the previous chapters. Consider these not as a set of instructions, but as possibilities to stimulate your thinking as to what you might do with your own learners. Just as every school and learner is unique, so is every educator. What matters most is that you find your own way with the shifts.

Microshift Ideas: Essential and Herding Questions

Essential questions are more than a school practice; they're a life practice as well. As our students begin to get ready for life outside of school, they will have questions—lots and lots of them. The biggest and perhaps most awe-inspiring one of all will simply be, What now? They can find out by quizzing themselves critically and thoughtfully about the things that are most important. It all comes down to asking the right questions. In addition to the microshifts I present in chapter 1 (page 9), here are several more microshifts of practice you can use to formulate better essential and herding questions.

Get Personal

Although we are leading our students toward understanding, they must also have self-knowledge and personal awareness in order to truly thrive beyond classroom walls. Present students with a questionnaire that highlights the exploration of their self-knowledge and awareness. Use questions like the following to really get to know your students and what their goals are, both for learning and for life.

- What is it most important for me to know about you?
- What are your personal values and beliefs about learning?

- What do you want to learn most? Least?
- How do you respond to challenges and problems?
- Who do you most look up to and why?
- What are your passions?
- What is it you need most from me?

Move the Herd

When we discover a truly essential question, it becomes easier to come up with different herding questions. We do this by connecting specifics that align with curriculum to the broader, less specific, and open-ended essential question. Find examples of essential questions and create as many herding questions from them as you can. Make this a class activity that you implement to connect to students' interests by using essential questions about topics that are of interest to them.

Encourage Essential Question Ownership

The teacher is the easiest source for answers, but redirecting the responsibility for finding that answer to the students will go a long way toward developing critical-thinking skills and fostering learning ownership. It's here we can use constructive redirection by showing students how to be the source of their own answers, with you guiding them along the way. When students ask about an essential question, encourage deeper thinking by asking them in return, "That's a very good question. What do you think? Where might you find your answer?" Lead them to consider how they could collaborate with others to find the solution.

Create a Dream State

The dream phase of solution fluency encourages us to *dream without borders* when visualizing solutions. You can get students asking good questions by placing them in these kinds of situations. Talk about issues that seem insurmountable. They could be something like pollution, poverty, or disease. It could be global warming or a dwindling water supply. It could be the effects of racism or war. These are all things we choose to think there are no solutions for. The whole idea of essential questions is exploring possibilities. It's about asking, "What if . . .?" Begin by asking students to forget what they think they know and think about the future. Have them imagine a tomorrow where these seemingly unsolvable issues are only distant memories. Encourage essential questions like the following.

- What does this impossible solution look like in practice?
- What would things be like if they got worse before they got better?

- What would the world be like if we actually made this happen?
- What would it take to create a global solution?
- How would our mindsets need to change to create a change for the better?

Bring in Bloom's

Our goal with learning is to provide students with activities that exercise skills found in the higher-end skills of Bloom's revised taxonomy (Anderson & Krathwohl, 2001). That said, the lower-order-thinking skills (remembering, understanding, applying) still have a place in learning, as they supplement the skills of analyzing, evaluating, and creating useful knowledge. Having a list of guiding questions for each stage can eliminate the dangers of flying blind when internalizing and using new concepts, and being able to refer to these resources can help such questions eventually become second nature. Break students into pairs or groups and help them collaborate on content-specific lists of the following: questions to help them analyze, questions to help them evaluate, and questions to help them create. They can use these lists anytime during a learning process and even turn them into resources they can share with others to maximize learning with Bloom's revised taxonomy (Anderson & Krathwohl, 2001).

Start WebQuests

WebQuests are exercises in which students use information-inquiry skills that involve gathering knowledge exclusively from the internet ("WebQuest," n.d.). It's a process that demands strong information fluency skills in the five As, in which essential and herding questions figure prominently. When you engage students in a WebQuest for knowledge about a certain topic, questions arise almost immediately. Learning how to ask the right essential and herding questions can yield more valuable information results during such searches. The better the quality and specificity of the search questions, the better the chance of learners finding useful information to answer questions and solve problems.

Divide the class into groups and give each group an exploratory essential question. The groups must go on a WebQuest to find as much information as they can to answer it. They will automatically employ herding questions in their respective searches for information. At the end of the class, have the groups share what they found out and explain why the information they discovered successfully answered their essential question.

Talk With Leaders

Students will be interested in science if they get to interact with subject matter experts, such as leaders working at a scientific laboratory or space center. They'll be more interested in politics if they can write to or even interview a state or local representative or mayor. You would be surprised how many important people are happy to communicate with schoolchildren on the day-to-day workings of their professions and the crucial issues they deal with on a regular basis. There are people in their fields of interest who are willing to answer well-developed questions and give some time to students who show genuine intrigue and a desire to learn. The more essential and carefully constructed students' questions are, the more likely they are to lead to effective herding questions. You can hold Skype conversations with local professionals in the community or beyond, meet them on field trips, or even arrange for them to visit the classroom. You might also consider asking students to contact officials from colleges or universities they want to attend. Encourage the students to ask these professionals tough questions.

Microshift Ideas: Connection Through Context and Relevance

Context and relevance provide solid connections for learners to engage with their own learning. In addition to the microshifts I present in chapter 2 (page 21), here are several more microshifts of practice you can use to engage your students.

Link to What's Local

Learning opportunities are everywhere in life if we can recognize them as teachable moments. Indeed, we can often link what we teach in our classrooms to what's happening in our communities. So much that is or can be of interest to learners is happening right outside our own doors. Being able to link events in our communities to students' in-class learning is a way to make learning relevant to them and place it within a familiar context. Find clear links between the lessons you design and events that transpire in your local community. Try lessons that can also get learners actively involved with individuals in the community.

Go on Field Trips

There is a reason why the good old educational field trip has never gone out of style. Still one of the very best ways to make learning interesting by providing clear connections to places outside school, field trips have gone virtual in the digital age. Global universities, businesses, landmarks, and other institutions are all available for students to fully experience using technology, without the hassle of bus rentals and permission slips. Physical field trips can, however, also get students outside of the classroom for a different perspective on learning, and the organization aspect of putting one together usually ends up being worth the effort because they end up enjoying themselves immensely and learning a lot in the process.

To help get your students engaged, discuss as a class what you'd like to do for your next field trip and even have students help organize it for a boost of responsibility and independent thinking. You can assign groups during the field trip to perform separate learning quests or lesson-related scavenger hunts as collaborative teams and introduce a little friendly competition into the mix.

Invite Guest Speakers

Another surefire way to help students make relevant connections to the world with learning is to bring in a guest speaker to share his or her experience and answer questions related to a class lesson. If it isn't possible to bring someone into class in person, another way to do it is virtually by way of Skype in the Classroom (https://education.microsoft .com/skype-in-the-classroom/overview) or other video-conferencing programs.

Arrange for a guest speaker to visit the classroom either in person or virtually in conjunction with one of your next lessons. Ensure that learners have worked on some relevant and interesting questions to prepare for the visit beforehand.

Get Hands-On

Touch is a powerful sense, and tactile sensations connect us to things in ways that our eyes and ears can't always achieve. As such, so many of our learners are kinesthetic learners. Being able to get their hands dirty creating and building something of value always gets students interested and engaged and is a great way to provide a different level of connection to learning.

Incorporate lessons into your timetable that allow students to build something physical, be they models or dioramas or actual working machines that serve a unique purpose or solve a specific problem. Because availability of classroom equipment is variable, creatively use whatever levels of tech you have on hand when determining what kinds of activities students can do.

Engage in Critical Reflection

Learning to question is undoubtedly a powerful way to make learning relevant. One habit we should strive to help our learners avoid is passively accepting information no matter what form it comes in. Information fluency and media fluency teach learners to actively and constructively scrutinize what they see and hear and to not simply take information and media messages at face value. Critical reflection on learning is an ongoing process that encourages students to ask questions for not only better learning but also improved social and cultural understanding and awareness.

Add critical reflection questions periodically throughout lessons and also afterward as part of the debriefing process. Encourage students to look beyond the immediate and perceive other issues, problems, and points of view that relate to the content and that help them achieve a deeper understanding of the social, cultural, and moral implications of the concepts they learn.

Share Some Stories

What tales of your own have you shared with your students? It's safe to say you've had plenty of life experience as a teacher that you can use to connect students to what you're teaching. In the process, you'll identify with them on a more profoundly personal and emotional level than you would simply delivering the content. Telling stories is one of the oldest forms of communication we have, and it can be surprising how interested our students are in hearing about the kinds of things we've experienced before, while, and even after we became teachers. Choose some interesting stories from your own background, career, or work that you can relate to the lessons you are using in class. Tell these stories to open up communication and sharing between yourself and the class to move learning forward.

Create Makerspaces

Makerspaces are not necessarily a new idea, but they have been making waves in education for their ability to engage digitally native students both intellectually and creatively in equal measure. A *makerspace* is essentially a collaborative working area that one can set up in a school or in a separate facility specifically for the purpose of engineering, exploring, and sharing real-world products and inventions created using high-tech, low-tech, or no-tech resources. Work with students and administrators to build and equip your own makerspace in or outside the school. There are lots of maker resources on the web to help you get started and maintain your space, including Renovated Learning (http://renovatedlearning.com/makerspace-resources), Smith System (https://smithsystem.com/smithfiles/2017/07/29/starting-a-makerspace-beginners-guide), Makerspaces (www.makerspaces.com), and Maker Share (https://makershare.com).

Microshift Ideas: Personalized Learning

Personalizing learning connects students with their own advancement. In addition to the microshifts I present in chapter 3 (page 35), here are several more microshifts of practice you can use to engage your students.

Give Students Some Choices

Allowing students some choices in how they approach a task or tackle an assignment is a great exercise in personal responsibility, time management, and independent thinking. One example is providing students with an activities list for the day and allowing them to choose the order in which they complete those tasks. Another way is beginning class with a roundtable discussion that encourages the students to clarify what they want to learn most from the day's or week's content.

Begin your class by asking the question, "What do you want to learn today and how?" Whatever the lesson content is for the day, this can also move into an exploration of learners' assumptions about the material.

Assess on the Go

Formative assessment is assessment *as* learning, which you can offer to students throughout the entire learning process in a variety of ways. You can use simple tools like formative feedback, discussion threads, peer-led quizzes, exit tickets, think-pair-share exercises, opinion charts, and many more. Any assessments you give should be goal oriented, actionable, and geared mindfully toward developing higher-order-thinking skills.

Choose one or two simple formative assessment tools to use for a few days with your classroom and carefully monitor the results. Use some of these ideas for inspiration.

Try Inquiry- and Project-Based Learning

There's nothing more effective at shifting responsibility from the teacher to learners than crafting challenges that require them to take on inspiring knowledge quests and engineer real products as solutions to real problems. Inquiry- and project-based learning were made for personalization. Designing solutions for problems that matter will call upon learners' individual skills and talents and have them working collaboratively and creatively to achieve the best possible learning outcomes.

The free version of the Solution Fluency Activity Planner (Global Digital Citizen Foundation, n.d.b) makes using this approach as part of your learning personalization plan easy, supportive, and enjoyable.

Let the Students Teach

Besides fostering valuable communication and instructive skills, letting students teach is a great ongoing formative assessment tool for gauging understanding and making learning personal. As a teacher, you know that if the learner can teach the content to others in a way that makes those learning from him or her not only comprehend it but benefit from it, then the student has it down. In addition, giving your natural instructors a chance to reinforce the concepts in themselves and in others by teaching it can be an inspiring moment in any classroom. Choose one or two students to teach a small portion of the material for the next few classes. Have them plan the progressions, the activities, and even the assessments for the rest of the students. Be on hand to guide them throughout the process and answer any questions.

Use Technology

Technology is not always necessary to make learning personal, but in my experience, it certainly helps. Inasmuch as teachers have high expectations of learners in any instructional area, the fact is that the learners also have high expectations of us. Inevitably, in any classroom setting learners will fully expect to be able to use the technology that they love and that is so central to their lives both in and out of school. Using their personal technology offers learners the chance to connect to instruction through tools and networks they find familiar and reassuring. Technology can also provide teachers with fast and effective ways to tailor instructional content and delivery methods for a wide range of learners, quickly locate resources for instruction, and build stronger relationships with their students.

Try incorporating technology into one or two classroom activities. You can, for example, use a social networking tool like Twitter (https://twitter.com) to do an in-class poll or host a quick quiz that learners tweet concise responses for.

Teach Digital Literacy

Modern learners require skills that include collaboration with both physical and virtual partners, media fluency, and digital citizenship. As learning becomes increasingly digital and the marketplace becomes more global due to the presence of technology, students will benefit from the kinds of knowledge that allow them to effectively navigate, analyze, utilize, and create information in a technology-driven world.

Have students create their choice of multimedia project to answer a practical challenge. Give them lots of room to be their creative selves and use media that speak to their interests and abilities. For example, they could create a webpage, develop a podcast episode, build a blog or a wiki page, film a video, produce an animation, or design a presentation.

Collaborate With Others

There's no question that incorporating personalized learning into your teaching practice can be overwhelming sometimes, and that's where your colleagues can come in. Building a network with a team of like-minded teachers to create divisions of labor can also give rise to fresh ideas and insights on how to best go about them. Teachers from diverse levels of experience and subject backgrounds will ease the burden of work, no matter if you collaborate with them personally or virtually.

Reach out to some colleagues or other teachers you know who have had experience with personalizing learning and ask them about their own experiences. Apply those experiences with your students.

Microshift Ideas: A Challenge of Higher-Order-Thinking Skills

By challenging your students, you engage their higher-order-thinking skills. In addition to the microshifts I present in chapter 4 (page 47), here are several more microshifts of practice you can use to get your students thinking at a deeper level.

Use Dynamic Debates

There's nothing like a good debate to get the blood flowing, and modern learners are passionate about many important issues that affect our world. Thus, they have equally passionate opinions. Class debates exercise your learners' organizational abilities and leadership skills and are useful for them to practice articulating in public speaking, building confidence, command of language, and many more qualities that are valuable to potential employers and postsecondary administrators. They take time and effort to prepare, but for activities that challenge learners to utilize higher-order-thinking skills in a competitive yet safe environment, class debates are a great way to go.

Discuss topics that cover a broad range of issues present in the world. Explore learners' assumptions about these issues, and decide on one that they are most passionate about. What is the one topic they'd all be interested in holding a class debate around? Once you and your students make that choice, organize a class debate around the subject that leads students to research the problem thoroughly, take a stand, defend that position, and offer challenging and relevant lines of questioning to the opposing viewpoints.

Form Forums

Discussion boards on every topic under the sun are all over the internet. They can be great sources of information and knowledge from participants with a wide range of expertise and interest in the focus topic. Although the lack of immediate, face-to-face responses and validation can put off many, the fact is that discussion boards offer space for conversations on topics to continue outside of class at a leisurely pace, and a way for less confident students to share their opinions with far less anxiety.

Encourage students to build discussion boards about in-class topics using a platform in which you can moderate comments and input as necessary.

Write Digital Stories

Exploring digital storytelling in your classroom connects students to an age-old practice in an entirely modern way that is relevant to them, namely by incorporating digital technology. Digital storytelling is a means for learners to engage in learning while exploring possibilities and harnessing creative potential. Storytelling is one of the greatest tools humanity has ever had for teaching and entertaining, and it comes with a healthy dose of critical-thinking and reasoning skills. When it comes to the art of digital storytelling, learners will also apply these skills to creating a visual product.

You can engage students in writing digital stories in a few different ways, and there are plenty of online tools learners can use to explore it, such as Storybird (https://storybird.com), VoiceThread (https://voicethread.com), and MySimpleShow (https://www.mysimpleshow.com).

Deliver a Persuasive Speech

Public speaking is a skill that lends itself to a broad range of situations in which being able to verbally express an idea or take an important stand can convert words into action. We use public speaking as much in small-group collaborations as we do when addressing entire nations of people. Think about the greatest and most moving public speeches in history and the people who made them great. Winston Churchill, Abraham Lincoln, Alexander the Great, and dozens more—what were the techniques and strategies these powerful public speakers used to create effective and memorable speeches? How could students use these very same tactics to compel an audience of their own?

Have students study famous speeches from history and use what they learn to write and deliver a dynamic speech of their own on a subject that they are interested in or concerned about. They should use techniques and strategies they learn from their study of some of the greatest speeches in human history and the people who made them great.

Invent Something Great

Every great invention in history started with a simple idea. The greatest minds of our time have always asked themselves, "How can we be better?" They looked at the world and saw something differently from the rest of us. What they see is a universal need to create or improve something in a way that enhances people's lives and makes the world a better place. What sorts of things do your learners believe people need or want to have drastically improved? When they look at a given situation or scenario, what do they see happening that could improve? When students do this, they can formulate their ideas into a concrete invention and explain it all in simple terms in a technical manual that explains what it would look like to someone seeing it for the first time.

Students can begin this activity by researching the whole process of bringing an idea for an invention from conception to physical reality. They should also research technical manual designs and possibly blueprint design so that they understand how people like engineers and inventors build things. Next, have them take on the role of an inventor as they conceptualize and design an idea for something that modern society could use to make people's lives a bit better or easier. Have them illustrate the invention's appearance and functionality in a technical manual.

Help a Charitable Case

Imagine a disaster that is broad in scope has just struck your community, leaving many people hurt and homeless. This scenario provides the perfect opportunity for your learners to spring into action to come up with ideas to help those in need. Their job would be to conceptualize and build a small volunteer organization from the ground up to combat the ill effects of this terrible tragedy. They would have to give their organization an identity, structure its workflow accordingly, consider what they want to accomplish, and support victims as a charitable organization. Are your students up for it?

Organize students into groups and have them research creating, developing, and operating a charitable organization. Using their knowledge, they will work in groups to design their own unique charity organizations for a fictional disaster in their community that has left people in need of help.

Dig Into the Webs of Time

Imagine Martin Luther King Jr., President Abraham Lincoln, Albert Einstein, Shakespeare, or Odetta Holmes having the same access to technology we have today. What if they all had websites? What could their genius and passion have accomplished that wasn't possible in their own time? How far could their voices have reached across the world, and how would their messages have changed?

Let students pick a moment in human history that defined an important figure from the past, and design a webpage from the point of view of that individual to share his or her ideals with a new generation. Encourage them to begin digging deep into the mind of an important historical icon and learn about his or her morals, values, and the message he or she worked tirelessly to bring to the world. How might they use the internet to spread their historical character's voice to a world that doesn't yet know how much it needs to hear it?

Microshift Ideas: Information Fluency for Research Skills

Students with a strong grasp of information fluency dramatically improve their ability to conduct research. In addition to the microshifts I present in chapter 5 (page 59), here are several more microshifts of practice you can use to get your students researching effectively.

Ask Purposeful Questions

When students conduct research for class projects, asking the most meaningful and deliberate questions possible is at the heart of successful information gathering. If their questions aren't focused on a keen exploration of the relevant topics, learners won't obtain the right information. If their questions aren't specific enough, they won't obtain enough information.

Lead students toward designing open-ended research questions around their content using *who, what, where, when, why,* and *how* approaches. The guides *Use These 5 Steps to Learn How to Ask Good Questions* (Crockett, 2017b), *25 Self-Reflection Questions to Get Students Thinking About Their Learning* (Crockett, 2017a), and *The Critical Thinking Skills Cheatsheet* (Crockett, 2016a) can show them how to formulate the most useful possible questions for their research.

Develop Research Teams

In classrooms and the workforce the world over, everyone achieves more by working together. Collaboration is a hallmark of the global digital citizen, and it happens with partners both in person and online. When working as a team on a project, members of the group can potentially achieve higher levels of productivity on the research component and yield more favorable results.

Organize your class into groups and assign topics to each group. Work with your learners to help develop a list of exploratory questions concerning what they want to find out about the topic and why. Next, guide them toward determining for themselves how they will collaboratively conduct the research component of this activity by taking responsibility for assigning roles and responsibilities among each member of the group. They will need to put a system of accountability in place for reporting and sharing their findings with the group and also outline clear milestones for measuring achievement.

Explore Fact and Opinion

When performing research tasks, learners will encounter many instances in which two opposing sides pit fact against opinion. Determining for themselves which is which, and clearly justifying their stand, is a terrific way for students to develop independent thinking and information-analysis skills.

Find or create a mixture of statements that are either fact or opinion and place them where the class can see and discuss them together. If it's a fact, have the learners vote with an *F* and then let them briefly explain how they can prove it. If it's an opinion, have them vote *O* and then briefly explain why they feel they can't prove it.

Tackle Some Trends

Being able to effectively evaluate trends can be a great critical-thinking exercise for your learners. At the beginning of the social media boom, trends were mostly focused on people and culture. With transparent online communication having globalized our marketplace, trend or data analysis is an advantageous practice for success in business, marketing, financial management, and other areas.

Conduct an open discussion about trends in your classroom and explore your learners' assumptions about them. Have them give specific examples of trends they follow and why they feel they are important.

Name Your Terms

When searching for information online, keywords and specific search terms can guide students' queries and help them find much more useful and relevant information for their projects. The more specific their search terms and keywords are, the better their results will be.

Break the class into groups and assign interesting and engaging topics to each group. Have them generate a list of specific keywords and search terms around that topic that are designed to help them answer specific questions you've created about it. Vary the level of difficulty of the questions the more your learners become successful in locating the information.

Use Social Media

Did you know it's possible for students to use social media as a classroom research tool? Over the years, social media has matured into a platform where people conduct real business in addition to making valuable connections to people, places, and information. As far as doing research is concerned, social media can assist students at every stage.

Assign research quests to your students in which they can only use social media to locate information. Set the specific goals for the research and establish the questions to ask. Students will then research and collect answers to the questions. Analyze and discuss them as a class to determine whether they answered the initial questions. Twitter, Facebook, and Pinterest are some good social media platforms to use for this microshift.

Cite Your Sources

When students use information they find online in their research projects, citing and crediting information sources properly is an integral practice that involves using information fluency. This trait is also a hallmark of responsible global digital citizenship, whereby we strive to practice respect and responsibility for others and their intellectual property. Properly recording all the sources they visit to obtain information for later referencing is a good habit for learners to get into. This will also help students when developing a bibliography for their projects or reports. There are several different ways to craft a bibliography, some for specific types of publications (Your Dictionary, n.d.). Having a general knowledge of these different methods will show students how easy it is to keep records of referenced information for their own protection and for the benefit and respect of its creators.

Hold a discussion with students about why it is important to properly cite all sources when researching and collecting information. Have them study how to cite for a bibliography from different sources such as books, websites, and articles.

Microshift Ideas: Process-Oriented Learning

Students with a strong grasp of solution fluency dramatically improve their abilities to engage in process-oriented learning. In addition to the microshifts I present in chapter 6 (page 75), here are several more microshifts of practice you can use to get your students researching effectively.

Choose Your Battles

As teachers, our ultimate goal is to give learners the tools they need to solve problems that truly matter on a personal, communal, or global scale. What they consider devoting their problem-solving capacity to and how they choose to conquer the challenges they face for the good of those affected define them both as people and as global citizens. When we guide them toward knowing the right choices based on moral and ethical practices, and provide the opportunity to make these critical assessments for themselves, we give them power and autonomy over their own learning and a sense of responsibility for themselves and others.

As individuals or in groups, ask students to imagine they have one problem that they could solve or one thing they could change—it could be personal, local, or global in nature. Encourage them to carefully consider their choice—what it could mean for themselves and for others, how they are choosing, and why. Ask them to create a detailed map of exactly how they would go about creating the solution to that problem using an essential fluency if every resource they needed was available to them. Whatever they choose, have them document their processes for later discussion.

Create Something New From Something Old

Creative minds are more welcome in business than ever. In fact, they are an essential part of designing and marketing a successful product. In his book *A Whole New Mind*, Daniel H. Pink (2006) states that the wealth of nations and the well-being of individuals depend on having artists in the room whenever they aim to design something. Creativity in business is about engineering consumer products that are practical, beautiful, and functional, and about dominating markets flooded with similar products using innovative designs that capture more attention and more consumer loyalty than their competition. But what about those product designs that never reach the wider market and never quite take off? What about older and more obsolete product designs? Is there a way to use the process of the five Is of creativity fluency to breathe new life into them?

Get students to research a failed or obsolete product of their choice and learn what they can about its history. Why did it fail? What is it about the functionality that didn't become something consumers need to have? How could they improve a product to make it more enticing, useful, and marketable? Let students use creativity fluency to redesign a failed or obsolete product for reintroduction into the mainstream market. They should thoroughly document their processes, be able to demonstrate what changes they made, and explain why they feel these changes are improvements that can benefit the target market.

Stimulate Inquiring Minds

We use information fluency for inquiry learning because its processes teach the full range of information literacy, from establishing the question to determining if we reached a satisfactory answer. We begin with questions instead of facts, and these questions drive the quest to expand our knowledge about a topic and contribute that knowledge to the development of viable solutions. As teachers, we assist discovery by helping to facilitate good questions that lead students to willingly explore a topic using their full capacity for curiosity and hunger for knowledge. The first step is finding out what is relevant to our learners and then forming inquiry questions around those interests.

Discover what your students are curious about and what they want to learn more about. Form essential questions around these topics and interests that guide them to ask more questions, seek more information, and come up with more answers. You can do this exercise individually, but it may be easier to have groups pick a topic that students can form questions around.

Build a Survival Kit

Digital citizenship is the practice of demonstrating respect and responsibility for oneself, others, and intellectual properties of all sorts in all digital environments. It pays to know how to keep yourself and others safe and secure in all online environments and how to show respect and consideration to the work of others. There are lots of tools and tips out there for students to find that can help them build digital citizenship survival kits as toolboxes to help them with their continuing digital citizenship practices. Aside from our own work at the Global Digital Citizen Foundation (https://globaldigitalcitizen.org), we recommend looking at the digital citizenship resources offered on Common Sense Media (https://www.commonsense.org/education/digital-citizenship). These kinds of resources can help them continue modeling exemplary behavior for living those parts of their personal and educational lives that happen in the digital world.

Have students familiarize themselves with digital citizenship practices. You can use my foundation's Digital Citizenship Agreements (Global Digital Citizen Foundation, n.d.a) to guide them. They can then source tools and resources to add to their survival kits that they believe will help them practice good digital citizenship as well as help them teach it to others. The components for their kits can include, but are not limited to, articles, infographics, podcasts, videos, worksheets, applications, presentations, and more. Have them share these kits with the rest of the class and explain why they chose the tools and resources they included.

Build a Class Agreement

At my foundation's website (www.globaldigitalcitizen.org), you can find a series of Digital Citizenship Agreements (Global Digital Citizen Foundation, n.d.a), which thousands of teachers all over the world use. Contained within these agreements are specific guidelines and tips for helping you and your students develop and maintain exemplary digital citizenship practices with technology, and also in personal interactions that happen both on- and offline. Codes of conduct and agreements such as these need not be strict sets of laws; rather, they can be positive and constructive pathways for students to learn to care for themselves and each other. How would your learners enjoy working together on an official class agreement outlining guiding principles for constructive behavior, interaction, and technology etiquette for the good of the whole class, and even the whole school?

Lead your learners in a discussion of what they feel are the most important values and ideals to have when it comes to interacting with others and conducting themselves in their learning environment. See if you can narrow it down to a list of distinctly different but equally valuable and practical points. Next, have learners draft these points into a class agreement to promote responsibility for themselves and for others. Have them place it on a poster that the entire class (or anyone who visits it) can clearly see.

Redesign the Learning Space

What makes a great learning space that's conducive to collaboration, focus, and productivity? What are the physical properties and spatial arrangements of the ideal learning space? Most of all, what kind of classroom would your students be excited to call their home for learning? Design thinking can play a significant part in engineering the classroom of the future. Chances are your learners have some innovative ideas for a cool classroom redesign, and they can use creativity fluency to expand on them.

Have students visualize and design their conception of an ideal learning space. Using either your existing classroom or another sample floor plan, guide them in the process of using an essential fluency to research, brainstorm, and create the ultimate innovative classroom. Focus on a space that is comfortable and practical and that fosters and promotes a healthy atmosphere for learning and instruction. They can present these projects in a digital format, make something more traditional, or even create a 3-D model or diorama.

Come From the Heart

Hunger and famine in different parts of the world are often far removed from our awareness. Distance and luxury can prevent us from having an understanding of the real suffering that is an everyday way of life for people in poorer regions. But occasionally, we get a glimpse of this tragedy through the heartfelt campaigning of organizations devoted exclusively to helping others worldwide.

Explain to students how, in our entertainment-obsessed culture, we tend to stand up and take notice when a popular celebrity adds his or her voice into the mix. Ask students to role play as a famous singer or songwriter who a charitable organization has asked to lend his or her voice to a campaign promoting the awareness of third-world hunger. Tell students the organization running the commercial has asked the singer to create a poetic verse to use as a voiceover for a special project that will promote awareness of the problem and inspire action to remedy it. Students should work in groups to research the background and nature of the situation, collect powerful images and film clips to create a one-minute campaign spot for television, and pair these stirring and emotional images with appropriate music and poetic verse in a voiceover. The organization the students are working for needs the final product in one week.

Microshift Ideas: Learning Intentions and Success Criteria

When students understand why they are learning what they are learning and what their goals are, they better understand the greater purpose of their work and how to achieve those goals. In addition to the microshifts I present in chapter 7 (page 91), here are several more microshifts of practice you can use to get your students researching effectively.

Post and Review Learning Intentions

When we talk about clear learning intentions, we of course mean transparency. Learners should be able to see through us and fully understand both what we want them to accomplish and what our assessment of their work will be based on. Without clarity and understanding, learners have nothing to strive for and no purpose for developing their own goals and milestones. To ensure this clarity, the first and most basic thing we can do is simply have an open discussion with them about the intentions and outcomes we have in mind, and the specific success criteria we've envisioned.

At the beginning of the lesson, place the learning intentions and the success criteria up where students can view and discuss them with you. This should only take about two or three minutes. Have students do their work and, at the end of the lesson, spend another two or three minutes reviewing the same criteria and ask learners to reflect on whether they accomplished the goals you set for them.

Co-Construct Success Criteria

When students have a chance to define their own success criteria, something magical happens. They suddenly have a bigger stake in the outcome, and their engagement comes from them striving to achieve it. It's almost like they're competing with themselves and challenging themselves to either meet or exceed the goals they've specified. This practice of co-constructing success criteria gives them a sense of responsibility for their learning in that it becomes more meaningful to them. They have a clear understanding of not only what they want to learn but why they want to learn it.

Put your learning intentions on display at the beginning of the class and then co-construct the success criteria with your learners. Afterward, as with the previous activity, perform a suitable debrief and reflection session with your students.

Engage Curricular Curiosity

Curricular objectives cover both an educator's *and* a learner's responsibilities for learning. Yet it's not very often that we share curricular objectives with our students, despite the fact that their classroom experiences strongly align to those objectives. Although a curricular objective's language can often be highly academic, your students can achieve a greater connection to those objectives by understanding how they may translate into something that makes sense to them. How might you and your learners work together to make curricular objectives a common language that they easily understand?

Put a curricular objective in front of your students and unpack it together into student-friendly language. Keep this new translation visible as a reference for periodically providing goals and setting expectations.

Establish Whys and What-Fors

One of the most common questions teachers face from learners concerns the purpose for the learning. More than ever, students struggle to understand the relevance learning has to them and their world. Looking at learning intentions through the lens of *why* and *what for* can make for some interesting conversation and can lead to the discussion of the deeper potential learning has to the world outside school; it's a connection our learners desperately want and need to make.

After you have discussed and clarified your learning intentions and criteria with your students, begin an open dialogue on why they think you are placing these concepts before them as learning tasks. Why do students think these are important concepts to learn?

Provide Learning Samples

By allowing students to view samples of work that pertain to the lesson at hand, we give them a sense of what we could expect from them in their own projects. Learning samples work to frame our intentions and criteria for students by giving them an idea of what they will be doing as tasks to demonstrate learning. Such samples can even help them develop and deliver criteria of their own.

Visual references have always worked wonders with students, and our digital-age learners are no exception. Provide curriculum-related samples of work of varying levels of quality to students and have them discuss the strengths and weaknesses of each piece. From there, allow them to design a basic framework for learning criteria on their own that you can all talk about and refine as a class.

Identify Four Outcomes

Even though our outcomes often represent meeting specific standards, we can also define outcomes by asking students a question: What do we want to achieve in this lesson? Since the outcomes you are striving for are already curricular in nature, learners' responses to this question can be personal achievements or conceptual skills. No matter what, establishing them firmly in the minds of your learners gives them something to shoot for, and gives relevance to the learning journey.

Identify four outcomes students need to achieve. Next, break students into four learning commons and have each group tackle one of these outcomes. When that is done, have the groups teach their respective outcomes to each other group.

Use Carousel Talk

Movement exercises are great icebreakers. Get-up-and-stretch physical activities get the blood pumping and the brain working. Movement also boosts enthusiasm. Use this microshift as a simple discussion tactic when students are helping devise learning intentions and success criteria.

In this activity, station large sheets of paper around the room with the topics *Learning Intentions* and *Success Criteria* at the top. Next, have student groups go around to each chart and brainstorm their ideas on the topic as if they were moving around in a carousel. When the carousel stops, as a class, have students discuss their ideas with you.

Microshift Ideas: Learner-Created Knowledge

When learners create, they are using the kinds of higher-order-thinking skills that will benefit them in their lives after school. In addition to the microshifts I present in chapter 8 (page 101), here are several more microshifts of practice you can use to get your students researching effectively.

Craft Photo Stories

Have you ever looked at a photo from a time before your own and wondered about the story behind it? What was going on when the photographer took the photo? Who were the people in it, and what was that momentary experience all about for them when it was captured on film? This is the kind of creative interpretation our learners can make by using their imaginations to tell unique and entertaining stories with historical snapshots as the perfect prompt.

Search for interesting open-source photographs from the past, and let your learners make their own interpretations about them that they can craft into stories and share with the class.

Reinvent the Wheel

Some inventions are a tremendous help to people and make our lives much easier but eventually outlive their usefulness. Ask your students, "What happens when an invention is past its prime?" Have them consider the question of whether there is any hope of breathing new life into it and bringing it to the public's attention once again as something that has value. This activity asks students to get creative by imagining new ways to make something old useful again.

Break students into groups and have them identify an invention or gadget that is no longer as useful to people or that is now obsolete. Encourage them to find a way to improve or redesign it to get it to work better and once again become useful to people. They should produce the redesigned technology invention or gadget using the resources available to them and also demonstrate the usefulness of the invention or gadget to include in an advertisement targeted to its intended audience.

Solve Ancient Mysteries

What is it about ancient, fantastical mysteries that many people find so intriguing? Folktales of restless spirits wandering old castles and lecture halls, artifacts of great historical significance discovered in the unlikeliest of places, unspeakable creatures roaming the forests of the south and the snow-capped mountains of the north, entire cities lost without a trace—the past is filled with legends of the unknown and unexplainable. It takes a lot of focused research and detailed investigation to bring the knowledge of these fascinating stories to the public.

In this activity, have your learners focus on a historical mystery and research to shed some light on it in their own unique and creative ways. Students should put together a special report on an ancient mystery in which they act as a team of special investigators who use research and a creative combination of filming, narration, imagery, animations, and staged interviews to bring their three- to five-minute presentation to life.

Be Tour Guides

Some people in the tourism industry hope that new mapping technologies might help boost tourism in areas where local economies depend on it. The idea is that taking virtual tours of these destinations increases people's desire to see the places in real life.

Ask your students how they feel their local community could boost its economy by attracting more tourists. Have them answer how they would go about it. Students should work in pairs or groups to create a guided tour of their town, city, or local area. They should map out absolute coordinates for each stop, write descriptions of each landmark, and use Google Earth (https://google.com/earth) to record the tour for prospective tourists.

Record Student Journals

The word *journal* is derived from the Old French word *jornel*, which literally means "a day's travel" ("Journal," n.d.). In addition to being excellent writing practice, journaling can help students record learning discoveries, brainstorm important concepts, and track their progress.

Have your students keep learning journals using tools they select from a list you set that allow them to record their thoughts and insights on class projects. Make sure the options you provide allow them to reflect on their own work and provide feedback to their peers. They should record in their journal their notes about the feedback they receive (both educator and peer feedback) and how they've incorporated it into their learning experiences. This kind of journaling allows them to track their own progress. You can also arrange to have one-on-one conferences with students to discuss questions they may have as they continually add to their journals.

Start a Health Hotline

Although dietary and health issues don't always rank that high on student priority lists, healthy lifestyles are important no matter what age you are. So, think about some ways in which you can instill health-conscious decision making into your learners. Encourage them to begin thinking of ways they can use technology coupled with personal knowledge to offer practical and useful advice on a wide range of health-related topics that their peers will find interesting and relevant. The idea here is to steer them toward discovering more and more about the benefits of making healthier lifestyle choices.

Let your learners show their ingenuity and concern for others by scripting and performing a five- to eight-minute video or podcast recording focused on healthy lifestyle choices for students. Have them produce their project in a manner that is informative, appealing, and relevant to a broad range of students.

Explore Our World Wonders

There are many geographical marvels that are renowned all over the globe. The majesty of Australia's Great Barrier Reef, the cascading beauty of Niagara Falls, and the arid expanse of Arizona's famous Grand Canyon are great examples. Many of these beautiful places are in danger of damage or destruction from severe environmental factors that often are a direct result of so many tourists coming to see them (Beach, 2017).

Ask your students how they might achieve striking a balance between a tourism trade that is continually building and expanding and the preservation of our natural landmarks. Have students share their ideas on how to preserve natural wonders by working together to create solutions for accommodating a growing number of tourists to a landmark in a way that protects it from further deterioration. They should design their recommendations to ultimately allow many people to continue enjoying these landmarks in the years to come.

Microshift Ideas: Mindful Assessment

Assessments need to be more than numbers. The best assessments are mindful tools that help drive and refocus learning to help students achieve their learning goals. In addition to the microshifts I present in chapter 9 (page 113), here are several more microshifts of practice you can use to get your students researching effectively.

Go Beyond the Test

Testing and quizzes are a necessary part of the school environment, but it's not enough to simply provide students with a percentage or a number. These sorts of summative assessments are mere snapshots of learning and are neither accurate nor effective ways to assess or summarize one's true learning capacity. Fortunately, there are many ways to transform a simple test into a richly collaborative learning activity. A simple shift in delivery of questions and student interaction can make all the difference.

Instead of having a formal test laid out, try presenting the questions one at a time, and allow students to attempt to answer. Next, break them into groups in which there's at least one student who understands the concept. Have these groups work collaboratively on an activity to reduce the gaps in understanding among peers. As you present the next question, you can assemble new groups.

Rethink Feedback

Part of being an educator is having the skills to make hard concepts easier to understand, and the ability to make all students feel accomplished no matter how much they're struggling. Giving learners feedback that enables and inspires them is an essential element in ensuring their growth. The feedback we give can potentially make or break a learner's interest in developing lifelong learning skills. Just as highly critical and negative feedback can be psychologically and emotionally debilitating and discouraging, great assessment feedback can push and inspire our learners to excel in ways they didn't know they could.

Experiment with answering these questions when designing feedback responses for your next lesson.

- What is my purpose in giving the feedback?
- What are the challenges with giving useful feedback?
- How can I address these challenges for the benefit of my learners?
- How will I move forward?

Likewise, asking the following kinds of questions before the work resumes can be very helpful with getting feedback from learners.

- Does this all make sense to you?
- Do you have any other questions or anything to add?
- Are you seeing some new possibilities for how you can move forward?

Conduct a Next-Step Activity

What if we allowed students to determine what's next for themselves after a lesson is done? Often, after a lesson has been particularly successful for students, they are inspired to go in a specific direction in terms of learning. In other words, they have a natural inclination to want to learn something specific or take a certain route to new knowledge. When students help drive their own learning they have a better chance of making progress.

Ask your students questions that focus on determining factors such as what they feel they did best, where they feel they could use the most improvement, what they are most curious about, what it would be most helpful for them to do next, and what activities they want to try to reach for their next-step goals. Work together with students on this to guide them in seeing where they may most need to improve, and allow them to think critically about how they want to make that happen.

Use Round-Robin Charts

The round-robin-charts strategy involves passing charts among groups to assess understanding. Round-robin charts are essentially collaborative charts students can use to share what they've learned with others, similar to a round-robin-style tournament in which all players take turns playing against each other. They can also share knowledge they have on a topic you covered with them in class.

Organize students into groups of four or five and have each group begin with a chart and some markers. The groups should record an answer to an open-ended question. Once the groups finish with their charts, they pass them on to the next group. Once every group has worked on every chart, discuss responses as a class.

Ask Strategic Questions

You can use strategic questioning strategies with individuals, small groups, or the entire class. Effective formative assessment strategies involve asking students to answer higher-order-thinking questions such as *Why?* and *How?* Higher-order-thinking questions require more in-depth thinking from the students and can better help the teacher discern the level and extent of the students' understanding than simple closed questions.

Use strategic higher-order-thinking questions as part of a verbal quiz on a topic of the students' choice. Instead of just accepting quick answers, encourage students to think about the deeper causes and workings behind a concept and to verbalize them for the class.

Write Three-Way Summaries

This strategy involves having students write three summaries of varying lengths on a topic. The idea here is to challenge them to use different modes of thinking and attention to detail. You can even have them target a specific platform or medium with each summary, such as Twitter, which will give them experience communicating messages with minimal wording and characters.

Individually or in groups, have students respond to a question or topic of inquiry by writing three different summaries for it: one that is ten to fifteen words long, one that is thirty to fifty words long, and one that is seventy-five to one hundred words long.

Implement Admission or Exit Tickets

A simple but effective formative assessment is the exit ticket or admission ticket. Exit tickets are small pieces of paper or cards that students deposit as they leave the classroom. Admission tickets, on the other hand, are something you have students do at the very beginning of the class.

Here is an example of how you can use admission or exit tickets in your next lesson: for exit tickets, have students write down an accurate interpretation of the main idea behind the lesson you taught that day. With that interpretation, they should provide more detail about the topic beyond what you specifically covered. For the admission tickets, have students respond to questions about homework, or on the lesson you taught the day before.

Microshift Ideas: Self- and Peer Assessment

When you involve learners in assessing themselves and each other, you increase their engagement and drive to self-develop. In addition to the microshifts I present in chapter 10 (page 121), here are several more microshifts of practice you can use to get your students researching effectively.

Use the Buddy System

In order to alleviate some anxiety about test taking, it's sometimes helpful to give learners a pretest preview. Think of it as the trailer for the upcoming feature-length test in which your learners can explore some of the concepts of the material the test covers with one or more of their peers. Obviously, this isn't graded, but it can help students learn from each other what holes they might have in their learning.

Have students partner up and test each other with preview questions that are part of an upcoming examination. These are basically warm-up questions to cover topics on the test. If plausible, students should be the ones to create these questions. They should discuss their answers with each other, focus on fundamental areas for improvement, and apply a plan of action for making that improvement happen.

Share Your Intentions

In any learning adventure, it's helpful to have both a destination and a road map to successfully get there. Learners desire to know what their goals are as much as they do why they are learning. One great way to ensure that happens is to allow them to get involved in making the decisions about what those goals should be. By giving learners a chance to help create their own learning intentions, we establish their trust and inspire their confidence. They also gain a fundamental understanding of what you expect of them and how you will assess their progress because they expect it of themselves. With this knowledge, learning and assessment both become deeply meaningful.

Before your next lesson, fully discuss the learning intentions and criteria for success you want to establish with your learners. Have them reflect on these goals and then offer any insights they have about what the criteria for meeting them should be and how they can determine them as a class. Give them some guidance as they develop these intentions and make sure that you all agree on them as being SMART learning goals (strategic and specific, measurable, attainable, results oriented, and time bound).

Let Students Lead

When discussing a book or idea, it's beneficial to have a student lead the discussion at times. It's a great way to enhance students' sense of responsibility for learning in a way that also develops leadership skills. It also demonstrates how well each student understands the curriculum. For example, the student in charge can ask questions of the other students that you as the teacher might not have thought of, leading to a much more organic and riveting discussion.

Ask different students to lead discussions and pose questions to the class about topics related to your curriculum. As the educator, you should still mediate the proceedings and keep a close eye on how things progress. Decide when to step in if the discussion becomes too visibly overwhelming for the student, or if a peer poses a question the leading student is struggling to answer.

Write a Test Question

Part of the way many students internalize learning is by asking questions to others as part of a review process. Such an activity can help them both assess what they've learned and contribute to others' understanding. You can engage students in this way by having them develop their own pop quizzes that they can pose to the full class.

At the end of a class or a lesson, have your learners generate one question related to content you covered during that lesson and provide the answer to it. Students should not show their questions or answers to any of their classmates. Then, have each student stand up and quiz the class with his or her question, comparing his or her own answer with those he or she receives from the class.

Be a Teacher for a Week

In a translation of the Chinese *Xunzi*, a philosophical text, we can find this phrase: "Not having heard something is not as good as having heard it; having heard it is not as good as having seen it; having seen it is not as good as knowing it; knowing it is not as good as putting it into practice" (Knoblock, 1994, p. 15). In other words, our best learning—as well as our learners' best demonstration of it—comes from application and practice. Many regard teaching as one of the toughest professions on the planet precisely because it takes true insight and understanding of a concept to be able to impart that same level of awareness to those who know nothing of the subject themselves.

Assign each student a few days or a week in which they get to act as the teacher for a set amount of time. This is something for which you should get students involved well in advance so they have plenty of time to prepare. Have them pick a concept or idea to show the class a little bit of each day for the time period you designated, but also be on hand to offer them insights on how best to do this. Help them with planning their lessons and preparing for their teaching spot so they can effectively explore an idea or concept.

Form Cooperative Learning Teams

Learning through collaboration is a hallmark of modern learners. Cooperative learning groups provide them with a support group that extends beyond the classroom and allows them more ways to progress and improve their learning.

Have learners form groups of three or four that meet one day a week outside of class using an online collaboration tool to review the ideas and concepts they have covered in class. In addition to reviewing content, they should tutor each other on areas where anyone may be struggling and perform their own quizzes and tests.

Talk It Out

Panel discussions offer a platform for students to openly discuss learning and clarify their understanding of everything from current events to units of exploration to what's happening in and around the school. Imagine hosting a talk show–style panel discussion in your classroom in which groups of learners stage their own creative self- and peer-assessment activity in the form of one-on-one or group discussions about the important topics you covered in class. Being able to discuss and review this content with their peers, ask each other questions about it, and challenge each other's viewpoints makes for lively learning in any classroom.

Break students into groups of three or four and have them create and host their own version of a talk show that discusses the subject-specific topics they are learning about in class.

References and Resources

Ackoff, R. L., & Emery, F. E. (1972). *On purposeful systems*. Chicago: Aldine-Atherton. As cited in Kirby, M., & Rosenhead, J. (2005). *IFORS operational research hall of fame: Russell L. Ackoff*. Accessed at http://acasa.upenn.edu/AckoffHallofFamefin .pdf on May 14, 2018.

Anderson, L. W., & Krathwohl, D. (Eds.). (2001). *A taxonomy for learning, teaching, and assessing: A revision of Bloom's taxonomy of educational objectives*. New York: Longman.

Australian Curriculum, Assessment and Reporting Authority. (n.d.). *General capabilities*. Accessed at www.australiancurriculum.edu.au/f-10-curriculum /general-capabilities on February 20, 2018.

Barrows, H. S., & Tamblyn, R. M. (1980). *Problem-based learning: An approach to medical education*. New York: Springer.

The Basics of Philosophy. (n.d.). *Constructivism*. Accessed at www.philosophybasics .com/branch_constructivism.html on May 7, 2018.

Beach, E. (2017, April 25). *How does weathering affect monuments?* Accessed at https://sciencing.com/weathering-affect-monuments-4324.html on May 8, 2018.

Black, P., Harrison, C., Lee, C., Marshall, B., & Wiliam, D. (2003). *Assessment* for *learning: Putting it into practice*. Oxford, England: Open University Press.

Black, P., & Wiliam, D. (1998). Assessment and classroom learning. *Assessment in Education: Principles, Policy and Practice, 5*(1), 7–74.

Bloom, B. S. (Ed.). (1956). *Taxonomy of educational objectives: Handbook I— Cognitive domain*. White Plains, NY: Longman.

Bob Lutz (businessman). (n.d.). In *Wikipedia*. Accessed at https://en.wikipedia.org /wiki/Bob_Lutz_(businessman) on February 20, 2018.

Briggs, S. (2015, March 7). *Deeper learning: What is it and why is it so effective?* Accessed at www.opencolleges.edu.au/informed/features/deep-learning on February 16, 2018.

British Columbia. (n.d.). *Core competencies.* Accessed at https://curriculum.gov.bc.ca /competencies on March 2, 2018.

Brookhart, S. M., Andolina, M., Zuza, M., & Furman, R. (2004). Minute math: An action research study of student self-assessment. *Educational Studies in Mathematics, 57*(2), 213–227.

Bruner, J. (1990). *Acts of meaning.* Cambridge, MA: Harvard University Press.

Buck Institute for Education. (n.d.). *About BIE.* Accessed at www.bie.org/about on March 2, 2018.

Campbell, D., DeWall, L., Roth, T., & Stevens, S. (1998). *Improving student depth of understanding through the use of alternative assessment* (Master's thesis). Chicago: St. Xavier University.

Chappuis, J., Stiggins, R., Chappuis, S., & Arter, J. (2012). *Classroom assessment for student learning: Doing it right—using it well* (2nd ed.). Boston: Pearson.

Crockett, L. W. (2016a). *The critical thinking skills cheatsheet* [Infographic]. Accessed at https://globaldigitalcitizen.org/critical-thinking-skills-cheatsheet-infographic on January 10, 2018.

Crockett, L. W. (2016b, August 2). *The critical 21st century skills every student needs and why.* Accessed at https://globaldigitalcitizen.org/21st-century-skills -every-student-needs on February 19, 2018.

Crockett, L. W. (2017a, November 6). *25 self-reflection questions to get students thinking about their learning.* Accessed at https://globaldigitalcitizen.org/25 -self-reflection-questions on February 19, 2018.

Crockett, L. W. (2017b, March 22). *Use these 5 steps to learn how to ask good questions* [Infographic]. Accessed at https://globaldigitalcitizen.org/ask-good-questions -infographic on February 26, 2018.

Crockett, L. W., & Churches, A. (2017). *Mindful assessment: The 6 essential fluencies of innovative learning.* Bloomington, IN: Solution Tree Press.

Crockett, L. W., & Churches, A. (2018). *Growing global digital citizens: Better practices that build better learners.* Bloomington, IN: Solution Tree Press.

Crockett, L. W., Jukes, I., & Churches, A. (2011). *Literacy is NOT enough: 21st-century fluencies for the digital age.* Thousand Oaks, CA: Corwin Press.

Dedrick, J., & Kraemer, K. L. (2017, November). *Intangible assets and value capture in global value chains: The smartphone industry.* Accessed at http://www.wipo .int/edocs/pubdocs/en/wipo_pub_econstat_wp_41.pdf on May 14, 2018.

Demirel, M. (2009). Lifelong learning and schools in the twenty-first century. *Procedia—Social and Behavioral Sciences, 1*(1), 1709–1716. Accessed at www.sciencedirect.com/science/article/pii/S1877042809003061 on February 19, 2018.

Dewey, J. (1933). *How we think: A restatement of the relation of reflective thinking to the educative process* (Revised ed.). Boston: D. C. Heath.

Dewey, J. (1938). *Experience and education.* New York: Collier.

Digital Promise. (n.d.). *Challenge based learning.* Accessed at http://digitalpromise.org/initiative/professional-services/challenge-based-learning on March 2, 2018.

Dugdale, A. (2010, April 20). *The young app-rentices: Five app developers ages 16 and under (update).* Accessed at https://fastcompany.com/1621539/young-app-rentices-five-app-developers-ages-16-and-under-update on January 11, 2018.

Dweck, C. S. (2006). *Mindset: The new psychology of success.* New York: Random House.

Educational Broadcasting Corporation. (2004). *Workshop: Constructivism as a paradigm for teaching and learning.* Accessed at www.thirteen.org/edonline/concept2class/constructivism on May 5, 2018.

Educational technology. (n.d.). In *Wikipedia.* Accessed at https://en.wikipedia.org/wiki/Educational_technology on February 16, 2018.

Falchikov, N., & Boud, D. (1989, December 1). Student self-assessment in higher education: A meta-analysis. *Review of Educational Research, 59*(4), 395–430.

Falchikov, N., & Goldfinch, J. (2000, September 1). Student peer assessment in higher education: A meta-analysis comparing peer and teacher marks. *Review of Educational Research, 70*(3), 287–322.

Global Digital Citizen Foundation. (n.d.a). *Digital citizenship school program.* Accessed at https://globaldigitalcitizen.org/digital-citizenship-school-program on January 11, 2018.

Global Digital Citizen Foundation. (n.d.b). *Solution fluency activity planner.* Accessed at https://globaldigitalcitizen.org/reimagine/solution-fluency-activity-planner on January 10, 2018.

Hanlon, M. (2008, December 24). *How iFart iPhone software makes US$10,000 a day.* Accessed at www.newatlas.com/how-ifart-iphone-software-makes-us10000-a-day/10616 on January 11, 2018.

Hattie, J. A. C. (2009). *Visible learning: A synthesis of over 800 meta-analyses relating to achievement.* New York: Routledge.

IB Group 4 subjects. (n.d.). In *Wikipedia.* Accessed at https://en.wikipedia.org/wiki/IB_Group_4_subjects#External_links on March 2, 2018.

iFart Mobile. (n.d.). In *Wikipedia*. Accessed at https://en.wikipedia.org/wiki/IFart _Mobile on February 27, 2018.

Immordino-Yang, M. H. (2015). *Emotions, learning, and the brain: Exploring the educational implications of affective neuroscience.* New York: Norton.

International Baccalaureate. (n.d.a). *Diploma programme.* Accessed at www.ibo.org /programmes/diploma-programme on February 27, 2018.

International Baccalaureate. (n.d.b). *The IB learner profile.* Accessed at www.ibo.org /benefits/learner-profile on February 20, 2018.

Jean Piaget. (n.d.). In *Wikipedia*. Accessed at https://en.wikipedia.org/wiki/Jean _Piaget#List_of_major_works on February 27, 2018.

Journal. (n.d.). In *Online Etymology Dictionary*. Accessed at www.etymonline.com /index.php?term=journal on January 11, 2018.

Jukes, I., McCain, T., Crockett, L. W. (2010). *Understanding the digital generation: Teaching and learning in the new digital landscape.* Thousand Oaks, CA: Corwin Press.

Kapor, M. (n.d.). Mitchell Kapor quotes. *BrainyQuote*. Accessed at https:// brainyquote.com/quotes /mitchell_kapor_163583 on January 10, 2018.

Khoso, M. (2016, May 13). *How much data is produced every day?* Accessed at www .northeastern.edu/levelblog/2016/05/13/how-much-data-produced-every -day on January 10, 2018.

Klingberg, T. (2009). *The overflowing brain: Information overload and the limits of working memory.* New York: Oxford University Press.

Knoblock, J. (1994). *Xunzi: A translation and study of the complete works.* Stanford, CA: Stanford University Press.

Kuncel, N. R., Credé, M., & Thomas, L. L. (2005, March 1). The validity of self-reported grade point averages, class ranks, and test scores: A meta-analysis and review of the literature. *Review of Educational Research, 75*(1), 63–82.

Lahey, J. (2014, October 15). *Get to know your teachers, kids.* Accessed at https:// theatlantic.com/education/archive/2014/10/kids-get-better-grades-when -they-share-similarities-with-teachers/381464 on January 9, 2018.

Lahey, J. (2016, May 4). To help students learn, engage the emotions [Blog post]. *The New York Times*. Accessed at http://well.blogs.nytimes.com/2016/05/04 /to-help-students-learn-engage-the-emotions on May 3, 2018.

Mabe, P. A., & West, S. G. (1982). Validity of self-evaluation of ability: A review and meta-analysis. *Journal of Applied Psychology, 67*(3), 280–296.

Maxwell, C. (2016, March 4). *What blended learning is—and isn't.* Accessed at www .blendedlearning.org/what-blended-learning-is-and-isnt on February 19, 2018.

McDonald, B., & Boud, D. (2003). The impact of self-assessment on achievement: The effects of self-assessment training on performance in external examinations. *Assessment in Education: Principles, Policy and Practice, 10*(2), 209–220.

Medina, J. (2008). *Brain rules: 12 principles for surviving and thriving at work, home, and school.* Seattle, WA: Pear Press.

National Governors Association Center for Best Practices & Council of Chief State School Officers. (n.d.). *About the Common Core State Standards.* Accessed at www.corestandards.org/about-the-standards on February 20, 2018.

New Zealand Ministry of Education. (n.d.). *Key competencies.* Accessed at http://nzcurriculum.tki.org.nz/Key-competencies on February 20, 2018.

Nielsen, J. A., Zielinski, B. A., Ferguson, M. A., Lainhart, J. E., & Anderson, J. S. (2013, August 14). *An evaluation of the left-brain vs. right-brain hypothesis with resting state functional connectivity magnetic resonance imaging.* Accessed at http://journals.plos.org/plosone/article?id=10.1371/journal.pone.0071275 on February 20, 2018.

Ogle, D. (1986, February). K-W-L: A teaching model that develops active reading of expository text. *Reading Teacher, 39*(6), 564–570.

O'Neill, J., & Conzemius, A. (2006). *The power of SMART goals: Using goals to improve student learning.* Bloomington, IN: Solution Tree Press.

Pink, D. H. (2006). *A whole new mind: Why right-brainers will rule the future.* New York: Penguin.

Rae-Dupree, J. (2008, April 6). Business looks for renewal in right-brain thinking. *The New York Times.* Accessed at www.nytimes.com/2008/04/06/business/worldbusiness/06iht-unbox07.1.11694141.html on January 11, 2018.

Ross, S. (1998, January 1). Self-assessment in second language testing: A meta-analysis and analysis of experiential factors. *Language Testing, 15*(1), 1–20.

Seeley, C. L. (2015). *Faster isn't smarter: Messages about math, teaching, and learning in the 21st century* (2nd ed.). New York: Scholastic.

Sensei. (n.d.). In *Wikipedia.* Accessed at https://en.wikipedia.org/wiki/Sensei on February 27, 2018.

Simon, C. A. (n.d.). *Using the think-pair-share technique.* Accessed at http://www.readwritethink.org/professional-development/strategy-guides/using-think-pair-share-30626.html on May 7, 2018.

Socratic seminar: Teacher and student guide. (n.d.). Accessed at https://lipscomb.edu/ayers/upload/file/66351/socraticseminarstudentandteacherguide.pdf on January 10, 2018.

STEM to STEAM. (n.d.). *What is STEAM?* Accessed at http://stemtosteam.org on March 2, 2018.

Straub, P. (2009, June 26). File:Sampleburndownchart.png. *Wikimedia Commons.* Accessed at https://commons.wikimedia.org/wiki/File:SampleBurndownChart.png on January 11, 2018.

Swenson, N. C., Picard, R. W., & Poh, M.-Z. (2010). A wearable sensor for unobtrusive, long-term assessment of electrodermal activity. *IEEE Transactions on Biomedical Engineering, 57*(5), 1243–1252.

U.S. Department of Education. (n.d.). *Science, technology, engineering and math: Education for global leadership.* Accessed at www.ed.gov/stem on March 2, 2018.

Vygotsky, L. S. (1978). Interaction between learning and development. In M. Gauvain & M. Cole (Eds.), *Readings on the development of children* (pp. 34–40). New York: Scientific American.

Wabisabi Learning. (n.d.). *Environmental solution fluency: GEMS Dubai American Academy.* Accessed at https://wabisabilearning.com/case-studies on May 9, 2018.

Wallace, C. (2016, September 2). *Obama did not ban the pledge.* Accessed at www.factcheck.org/2016/09/obama-did-not-ban-the-pledge on February 26, 2018.

WebQuest. (n.d.). In *Wikipedia.* Accessed at https://en.wikipedia.org/wiki/WebQuest on March 1, 2018.

Wells, R. (1998). The student's role in the assessment process. *Teaching Music, 6*(2), 32–33.

Wiggins, G. (1990). *The case for authentic assessment.* (ERIC Document Reproduction Service No. ED328611). Accessed at https://files.eric.ed.gov/fulltext/ED328611.pdf on May 16, 2016.

Wiggins, G., & McTighe, J. (2005). *Understanding by design* (Exp. 2nd ed.). Alexandria, VA: Association for Supervision and Curriculum Development.

Wiliam, D. (2018). *Embedded formative assessment* (2nd ed.). Bloomington, IN: Solution Tree Press.

Wineburg, S., McGrew, S., Breakstone, J., & Ortega, T. (2016). Evaluating information: The cornerstone of civic online reasoning. *Stanford Digital Repository.* Accessed at http://purl.stanford.edu/fv751yt5934 on January 10, 2018.

World Wide Web. (n.d.). In *Wikipedia.* Accessed at https://en.wikipedia.org/wiki/World_Wide_Web on January 10, 2018.

Your Dictionary. (n.d.). *Bibliography examples.* Accessed at http://examples.yourdictionary.com/bibliography-examples.html on May 7, 2018.

Zehr, H. (1990). *Changing lenses: A new focus for crime and justice* (3rd ed.). Harrisonburg, VA: Herald Press.

Index

"Many teachers appreciate that teaching literacy skills is not enough to equip and empower the modern-day learner but remain uncertain about what and how to change. The result is to default to conventional practice. In Future-Focused Learning, Lee Watanabe-Crockett provides the toolkit for teachers to move from proficient to dynamic in order to equip and empower the modern-day learner. It makes the overwhelming become achievable by providing practical guidance for teachers to shift their practice in gradual steps."

—Marcus Knill
Principal Consultant, Department for Education, South Australia

"While others still debate what a 21st century curriculum is, Lee Watanabe-Crockett brings educators on a journey from why to how, from fluencies to shifts of practice. It's a journey through which educators can use a highly effective method of engaging learners in complex thinking to achieve outcomes thought unimaginable only a few years ago."

—Simon McGlade
Principal, Newport Gardens Primary School, Newport, Australia

"*Future-Focused Learning* will take a school or division on a journey away from initiative fatigue and toward a transformation of practice and learning. It's an excellent choice for a staff book study, as the ideas Lee Watanabe-Crockett presents apply and connect to all subjects in any school interested in an intentional, collective, and collaborative pathway toward change. A must-read for any educator!"

—Evan Robb
Principal, Johnson-Williams Middle School, Berryville, Virginia

"*Future-Focused Learning* succinctly summarizes the key shifts happening in education. With a focus on the practitioner, the chapters offer practical suggestions, tools, and activities to nudge educators to embrace these shifts as opportunities to propel their practice."

—Rebecca Stobaugh
Coauthor, Real-World Learning Framework for Elementary Schools

"In this book, Lee Watanabe-Crockett continues to focus on the how not just the why when designing instruction for contemporary classrooms and schools. The ten shifts and the microshifts in this book will inspire all future-focused educators to take the next step in their own professional transformation. Educational leaders should view this book as a road map to influence teachers and motivate modern learners."

—Jackie Vaughan
Deputy Principal, Canberra, Australia

Growing Global Digital Citizens
Lee Watanabe-Crockett and Andrew Churches
Discover how to transform education through the concept of global digital citizenship (GDC). Embraced by thousands of schools, GDC practices empower students to effectively and ethically participate in and contribute to the digital world around them.
BKF786

Mindful Assessment
Lee Watanabe-Crockett and Andrew Churches
It is time to rethink the relationship between teaching and learning and assess the crucial skills students need to succeed in the 21st century. Educators must focus assessment on mindfulness and feedback, framing assessment around six fluencies students need to cultivate.
BKF717

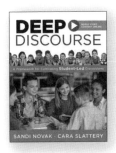

Deep Discourse
Sandi Novak and Cara Slattery
When educators actively support student-led classroom discussions, students develop essential critical-thinking, problem-solving, and self-directed learning skills. This book details a framework for implementing student-led classroom discussions that improve student learning, motivation, and engagement across all levels and subject areas.
BKF725

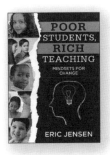

Poor Students, Rich Teaching
Eric Jensen
Discover research-based strategies to ensure all students, regardless of circumstance, are college and career ready. This thorough resource details the necessary but difficult work that teachers must do to establish the foundational changes that positively impact students in poverty.
BKF603

Solution Tree | Press
a division of
Solution Tree

Visit SolutionTree.com or call 800.733.6786 to order.

Wait! Your professional development journey doesn't have to end with the last pages of this book.

We realize improving student learning doesn't happen overnight. And your school or district shouldn't be left to puzzle out all the details of this process alone.

No matter where you are on the journey, we're committed to helping you get to the next stage.

Take advantage of everything from **custom workshops** to **keynote presentations** and **interactive web and video conferencing**. We can even help you develop an action plan tailored to fit your specific needs.

Let's get the conversation started.

Call 888.763.9045 today.

SolutionTree.com